Mothers Unite!

Mothers Unite!

Organizing for Workplace Flexibility and the Transformation of Family Life

Jocelyn Elise Crowley

ILR Press
an imprint of
Cornell University Press
Ithaca and London

First published 2013 by Cornell University Press

Printed in the United States of America

Library of Congress Cataloging-in-Publication Data

Crowley, Jocelyn Elise, 1970–
    Mothers unite! : organizing for workplace flexibility and the transformation of family life / Jocelyn Elise Crowley.
        p. cm.
    Includes bibliographical references and index.
    ISBN 978-0-8014-5175-1 (cloth : alk. paper)
    1. Mothers—United States—Societies and clubs.
    2. Women employees—United States—Societies and clubs.
    3. Work and family—United States.   I. Title.
    HQ759.C94   2013
    306.874'3—dc23   2012042157

Cornell University Press strives to use environmentally responsible suppliers and materials to the fullest extent possible in the publishing of its books. Such materials include vegetable-based, low-VOC inks and acid-free papers that are recycled, totally chlorine-free, or partly composed of nonwood fibers. For further information, visit our website at www.cornellpress.cornell.edu.

Cloth printing   10 9 8 7 6 5 4 3 2 1

For Alan, Monica, and my mother,
with incredible gratitude

Contents

Acknowledgments

I started thinking about writing this book when I was reflecting on a particularly vivid memory from my childhood. My mother was a single parent, working two jobs (including weekends), and going to school in the evenings. Money was very tight then, and I remember that she had no access to paid time off in case my sister or I became ill and had to be pulled out of elementary school. I did not want to put additional stress on my family, so I tried very hard not to get sick. In my child's mind, I feared that if my mother lost an afternoon's wages picking me up from school, we might not have food on the table that night. That scare, that fright, has stayed with me until this day. This book aims to do something positive with those powerful, lingering emotions for all mothers and their children in the twenty-first century.

I thank the financial supporters of this project, without whom this book would have simply remained ideas loosely organized in my head. Thanks most of all to Kathleen Christensen at the Alfred P. Sloan Foundation for guiding the project to fruition. The Michael J. and Susan Angelides Public Policy Research Fund at the Edward J. Bloustein School of Planning and Public Policy at Rutgers was extremely generous in supporting the transcription of all the interview recordings included here. In addition, I benefitted from several Rutgers University Research

Council grants, which helped with multiple parts of the project. Raymonde Pozzolano and her team offered excellent transcription services, as usual.

I am extremely grateful to the five mothers' organizations that are the subject of this book. Their leadership were kind enough to provide me with access to their membership and trusted me to tell their stories accurately. The mothers who actually participated in the study, by being observed, interviewed, or surveyed, also gave generously of their time. I learned so much from them, and they have changed my perceptions about the challenges of motherhood forever.

I am also grateful to the staff at Cornell University Press. My editor, Frances Benson, believed in the project from the beginning and helped guide it seamlessly to publication. Kitty Liu answered all my annoying editing and production questions without complaint. Special thanks to Susan Specter and Romaine Perin for their excellent copyediting skills. Of course, the anonymous referees greatly enhanced the value of the work across each chapter.

Personally, I wrote this book during a time in my life that was incredibly challenging. It helped to remember that, as I heard the television character Dr. Gregory House advise, "People get what they get. It has nothing to do with what they deserve." In addition to the help of a fictional protagonist, numerous real-life people supported me through this process. First of all, my colleagues at Rutgers went above and beyond the call of duty in helping me with this effort—Dr. Marc Weiner and Dr. Kelly Dittmar in particular—I am looking at you! Liza Viana, Melissa Chedid, and Vanessa Alger also provided excellent research support. Second, my friends and close family built a firewall around me as I continued to write. Maryann Barakso, Elizabeth Wood, Theresa Luhm, Amy Schapiro, Sandhya Higgins, Ellen Braitman, John Spry, Michelle Wilson, Susan Crawford Sullivan, Suzanne Glaser—thank you for listening. You constantly pointed to the light at the end of the tunnel that on many days I could not see. Most important, my mother, my sister Monica, and my husband did incredible amounts of hand-holding as I assembled the manuscript. I cannot thank them enough, and I dedicate this book to them. And, of course, M. B. Crowley's support never wavered. Don't worry, my precious angel, I will see you soon.

Mothers Unite!

1

American Mothers, American Troubles

After graduating from Harvard Law School in 1988, a young woman named Michelle joined the law firm of Sidley Austin in Chicago, where she specialized in corporate transactions. The job offered more than an introduction to the complex world of legal analysis and maneuvering. When a handsome young summer associate came to work there, it took her only a little while to realize that she had met her romantic match.

With a partner whom she eventually married at her side, Michelle saw her career begin to rise as she moved on to challenging new opportunities. In 1991, after leaving Sidley, Michelle went to work for the Chicago mayor's office; there she helped promote urban economic development in underserved neighborhoods. She then moved on to the Chicago Transit Authority to become head of the citizens' advisory board. Later, she ran the nonprofit organization Public Allies, which trained young people for careers in public service by helping them secure internships. Following that experience, she went to the University of Chicago, taking a job in student services and initiating a new community-based program in order to enhance city-college interactions. By 2005, she had become vice president for community and external affairs at the University of Chicago Medical Center.

These career moves all ended in 2007, when the handsome young associate with whom she had fallen in love years ago at Sidley Austin—a man named Barack Obama—decided to run for president. With two young daughters, Malia, born in 1998, and Sasha, born in 2001, Michelle took a leave of absence from her job to help her husband campaign. When he became president, she permanently quit her paid job and declared her new employment intention to be mom in chief to her daughters.[1]

Michelle Obama's story is, in many ways, a common one: that of the modern American middle-class mother. Each part of her tale resonates with some trace of who we were in the past and who we are now. That is, some of us can relate to the young woman, fresh out of school, trying to make a name for herself in the competitive professional world. Others are drawn to her quest to fulfill her true passions, whether they be in the corporate or nonprofit world. Still others focus on, ponder, celebrate, and critique her decision to devote herself to her family in recent years by dropping out of the paid labor force.

Perhaps, though, what is most compelling about Michelle's story is that it is intriguing not only because of these distinct *parts* of her life but also because of the compelling push and pull of the forces that emerged over the *complete trajectory* of her evolution as a modern woman. She faced decisions that many middle-class mothers must confront as they experience the birth and then the numerous stages of their children's development. When, exactly, should they have children? If they are working, how much time should they take off? Should they even return to the paid workforce at all? If they do return to work, who will take care of their children? Can they even afford not to work? What is the best arrangement for them, their families, and their children? How do they know that they have made the right decisions?

What is also compelling about Michelle Obama's life course is that it truly mixes the complex reality of *personal* and *public* decision making regarding if and how mothers pursue paid work in the United States. In this context, *personal decision making* means the range of individual choices mothers have within their reach about the future of their lives. Clearly, mothers make decisions about their educational and occupational pursuits all the time. With more resources at their disposal, such as a higher socioeconomic status and networking connections, many mothers have a broader array of choices that they can pursue. They can work in a demanding field, work part time, or not work for pay at all. They can purchase services that help them manage their lives, services such as high-quality child care and housekeeping assistance. Yet their stress levels may still be high. Isolation, if they elect to stay at home, and feelings of being overwhelmed by paid work and family responsibilities, if they remain employed, are commonplace among this group of mothers.

Mothers with fewer resources on hand still have the ability to make personal decisions about paid work, but their choices are much more limited. Because they earn lower wages, staying at home with their children may not be financially possible. The jobs that they hold are likely to have few, if any, benefits and to require unpredictable or irregular hours. On the other hand, since child care costs are likely to be proportionately very high if they were to work in a low-wage job, staying at home might be the only option that they have. They would then need to rely on a partner, other family members, or public benefits in order to pay their bills. For these mothers, then, psychological, emotional, and physical strains can quickly emerge under the best of conditions.

Regardless of socioeconomic status, most mothers still struggle with whether the arrangement that they have ultimately established is most suitable for their families. Guilt on all sides runs rampant. Yet all of these mothers' arrangements are debated by media pundits in a very different way under the label of the "Mommy Wars." In this oversimplistic narration, personal decisions about a mother's level of paid labor force participation are not complex all. Instead, they are made by one-dimensional characters who believe either that working for pay is better or that staying at home is better. Anyone who makes a decision that does not mirror her own is a "bad mother."

While mothers with many and those with limited resources are both able to exercise a certain degree of personal autonomy over the structure of their work and family lives—and the media's portrayal of the Mommy Wars almost exclusively focuses on these individual "choices"—it is important to recognize that public decision making can also expand or contract the scope of power they have over the nature of the paid work options they face as well. In this context, public decision making pertains to the range of opportunities and actions offered by firms, organizations, and all levels of government that can influence individuals' lives. These can include critical initiatives in the form of child care options, health care benefits, and other types of employee assistance. However, in this book I am concerned with one central aspect of public decision making as it affects mothers' opportunities in particular: workplace flexibility policy. And I ask a series of fundamental questions related to the potential for political activism to emerge on this issue: do women want to come together to build a new mothers' movement on behalf of promoting more flexible work options? Can they? Should they?

What Are Workplace Flexibility Policies?

Simply put, workplace flexibility policies are any initiatives that provide workers with options regarding the structure of their work lives. More concretely, workplace flexibility can be broken down into three critical areas: flexible work arrangements; time-off options; and career exit, maintenance, and reentry pathways.[2]

Flexible work arrangements represent the first component of workplace flexibility. When these options are in place, employees exercise some control over the timing of their work day, their location of work, or both. Concrete examples include the provision of alternative work schedules (i.e., nontraditional start and end times or compressed workweeks) and advanced knowledge of overtime possibilities, predictable scheduling, and defined break schedules. Part-time work, job shares, or part-year work are also part of flexible work arrangements. Last, workers may also have the opportunity to work at home or at an alternative location. Research has consistently shown the benefits to workers of these policies. For example, employees are more likely to be engaged and satisfied with their jobs when they are granted these new options to manage their work time.[3] Flexibility can also substantially decrease stress and burnout among workers and can actually improve concrete measures of physical health, such as lowering cholesterol levels. Health outcomes are thought to improve because workers have a greater sense of control over how their lives are scheduled in their totality.[4] Finally, employees are likely to have lower degrees of work-family conflict and an increased sense of work-family balance, possibly also because of their enhanced autonomy over the management of their time.[5]

Time-off options represent the second element of workplace flexibility. Guaranteed short-term time off, for example, provides workers with the ability to properly respond to planned or unplanned events. Examples include attending a child's school event, taking care of a personal illness, and addressing the illness of a loved one or a medical or home emergency. Also under this category are both episodic time off to handle recurring appointments or life issues (medical treatments, community service, advanced education) and extended time off to deal with an issue that lasts longer than five days but less than one year (taking care of a child or loved one, having a severe health issue, serving in the military). Shorter time off is beneficial for all workers, but especially for those working in low-wage jobs; those on the bottom rungs of the employment ladder in particular have little room in which to adjust their schedules to meet their own as well as their families' medical needs.[6] Of course, for longer periods of time off, the United States has in place the Family and Medical Leave Act, which provides up to twelve weeks of unpaid leave for workers in organizations with fifty or more employees. For those workers who do qualify, this leave, and probably leaves like it, enable mothers to return to their jobs without significant wage and career advancement penalties.[7]

Career exit, maintenance, and reentry pathways represent the last component of workplace flexibility. Workers use these policies to either decelerate or accelerate their careers when confronted with severe or time-consuming changes in their lives, such as new caretaking responsibilities or health care needs.[8] Examples of exit and maintenance strategies would be opportunities for part-time work and continued education. Reentry pathways would include employer initiatives such as the active recruitment of those workers who may have been out of the workforce for a significant period or the creation of job fairs in areas where underrepresented workers live. These types of policies are especially important to mothers, who may prefer working part time to not working at all. Mothers also might have substantial gaps in their résumés if they have taken months or years off to raise their children.[9]

While there are clear benefits to employees from having workplace flexibility, research has documented significant gains to employers as well. More specifically, workplace flexibility options are central to attracting the best possible talent to a set of jobs.[10] Not surprisingly, good workers want to be where such options are offered, valued, and supported. By extending such options, employers gain employees who are more committed to their work and, hopefully, are therefore able to retain them for longer periods of time. This retention is essential because the cost of finding new employees can be excessively high.

Implementing advertising strategies, deploying headhunters, using human resource managers, and retaining relocation-assistance consultants can all cost firms significant resources. It makes sense, therefore, for firms to try to avoid these expenses. Indeed, research has documented that companies tend to retain strong talent when they create specialized initiatives that assist mothers who are temporarily leaving work and planning to return a short time later.[11]

Employers also obviously care about absenteeism. Without dependable workers able to execute the tasks of their jobs on a daily basis, firms suffer in terms of their bottom line. This can be especially true for small companies, for which any missing worker can cause a disproportionate impact on productive output. While workers can be absent for various significant reasons, happiness and a sense of well-being at their place of employment can prevent unnecessary days off. Again, here, too, it makes sense for employers to be attentive to the workplace environment. Indeed, several studies have indicated that firms that offer more flexibility options have lower rates of absenteeism than those that do not.[12]

Yet American work culture is difficult to change, and employers have vocalized concerns about these policies.[13] Many supervisors have grown up in a context in which all their employees are expected to be "ideal workers," dedicated and available to their jobs 100 percent of the time.[14] Believing in this ideal-worker ideology, these employers fear the reactions of their customer base should their workers not be physically present on a consistent, "traditional" basis. Some types of jobs may be ill suited for flexibility, for example, when employees must work as a team on a similar schedule toward a common goal. Furthermore, there are employers who are afraid of employee abuse of these new options and of their inability to properly monitor worker activities. Small businesses in particular may be wary of any type of time-off policies or worker exit and reentry policies because of the costs they might face in either holding jobs for these employees or in training new workers.

These fears are reflected in the relatively low levels of flexibility employers currently offer their employees. According to the 2008 Study of Employers by the Families and Work Institute, a nonprofit organization dedicated to generating research about the modern, changing workplace, employers vary to an extraordinary extent in what they are willing to consider offering in terms of flexibility. For example, concerning flexible work arrangements, while 79 percent of employ-ers allow at least some of their employees to vary their start and stop times, only 23 percent permit employees to work at home for part of the day. Likewise, for time-off options, 73 percent of employers permit some of their employees to take time off during the day to attend to per-sonal matters, without pay, but only 47 percent allow their workers to engage in voluntary work during the work day. Finally, with respect to career exit, maintenance, and reentry, 74 percent of employers consent to some of their employees taking paid or unpaid leave to improve their educational level or skill set, but only 38 percent will provide some of their employees with a sabbatical from work (six months or more) and a guarantee to return to a comparable job.[15] It is critical to note that these statistics also reflect employers' reporting that they offer these benefits to "some" of their employees. When employers are asked if these op-tions are offered to "all or most" of their employees, these numbers drop dramatically. Overall, these statistics demonstrate that there is clearly room for a dramatic expansion in workplace flexibility options for the great majority of American workers.

It is also important to note that to the extent that flexibility exists, it is primarily a benefit for workers with higher levels of education. This is true for several reasons. First, employers frequently view flexibility as a form of compensation, and thus the higher the level of education an employee has (and therefore the higher the level of his or her pay), the more likely that worker is to receive flexibility. Second, employers often have concerns about giving lower-wage workers flexibility due to fear of increased management costs. For example, in the retail or food sectors, personnel must be reliably on hand to meet the needs of a steady stream of consumers. When workers have flexibility, supervisors need to expend extra effort in making sure that schedules are covered. Overall, though, regardless of a particular employee's level of education, workplace flexibility is clearly not a possibility for sizeable numbers of American workers.[16]

In addition to differences in who are actually offered these policies, there are disparities in policy uptake. On this point, studies have shown that men and women use flexibility policies at different rates. While there are many similarities between men and women—for example, re-search has shown that at incomes lower than $25,000 men and women use flextime at about the same rate—at higher levels of income, the sexes diverge. More specifically, men are more likely to use flextime when family incomes range from $25,000 to $74,999; interestingly, women assume higher rates at family income levels at $75,000 and above.[17] Other scholarship suggests that men and women use flexibility policies at the same rate when they are childless or have adult children, but that women are more likely to use a subset of them such as job sharing, telecommuting, part-time work, and flextime when there are young children present in the home.[18]

While flexibility might be offered on paper, workers might be hesitant to use it. In fact, there is a strong work culture that promotes the notion of the ideal worker in the United States; this is the type of employee referred to earlier, heavily committed to her job and available to her supervisors twenty-four hours a day.[19] So, companies may have both formal and informal policies that supposedly encourage flexibility, but workers may fear using them if they perceive that they will encounter some type of harm to their career in doing so, such as pay and promotion penalties. Flexibility policies must be viewed by workers as usable, without any supervisor retribution, for them to be helpful, but the reality is that many workers shy away from even broaching the topic within their organizations.[20]

But what if mothers could come together as a unified group and demand flexibility? In this book I examine the interesting phenomenon of women joining the largest and most influential mothers' organizations in the United States, groups that, although presenting different approaches to the issue of workplace flexibility, all implicitly or explicitly endorse it. Not surprisingly, groups with a higher percentage of mothers who work for pay tend to stress in their policy positions an activist role for firms and the government regarding workplace flexibility, while groups with more stay-at-home mothers tend to advocate more individual responsibility in establishing satisfactory work-life arrangements. Despite these public positions, however, little is known about group members' true opinions on this critical employment issue. The puzzle that I seek to solve is whether support for workplace flexibility as a general principle can unite members across these divergent groups, potentially creating a viable mothers' movement. If so, all these groups can then become vehicles for mobilizing action as they strive to make the lives of all American mothers more productive, sustainable, and meaningful over time.

Why Study Mothers Organizing in the United States?

The groups that are the focus of this study include Mothers of Pre-schoolers (MOPS), Mocha Moms, Mothers & More, the National Association of Mothers' Centers (NAMC), and MomsRising. Each group will be described in detail over the course of the next several chapters. First, however, it is important to lay out the proper contextual foundation for studying them. There are two main issues at stake: why this book focuses on *mothers* rather than both *fathers and mothers*, and why it examines *mothers' groups* in particular rather than *parents' groups*.

Workplace flexibility clearly affects both parents—mothers and fathers—and their ability to lead happy, satisfying lives. And undoubtedly, fathers have become more involved in raising their children over time, making workplace flexibility a critical issue for them as well. However, biology still demands that mothers carry children during pregnancy, and a significant number of mothers want to breastfeed after their babies are born. These realities require that mothers remain with their children for an extensive period after birth. Moreover, although fathers are contributing greater levels of care to their children, mothers still carry the disproportionate burden of responsibility in this area even after the breastfeeding years are over. On average between 2005 and 2009, for example, while fathers spent 1.22 hours a day doing household chores, mothers spent 1.98 hours. Mothers also spent 1.24 hours a day on helping and caring for household members, including children, in contrast to .87 hours a day for fathers.[21] With family demands more predominantly experienced by them, then, mothers are more likely than fathers to press for change in the area of workplace flexibility. It is for these reasons that I examine mothers rather than both parents as agents of transformation in the realm of workplace flexibility. I also focus on mothers' groups in particular rather than parents' groups as the locus of such change. And why? Collective action in the form of group initiatives drives the restructuring of life in American politics. But notably, mothers more frequently than fathers organize in American politics in their role as parents. In fact, mothers organizing with one another on behalf of shared goals has a rich history across the American political landscape.[22] In some cases, their campaigns have been very loud and visible, while in other cases, their mobilizing efforts have been more quiet and behind the scenes.

What were the largest and most geographically expansive mothers' groups that preceded those studied in this book?[23] And what can be learned from them in their attempts to effect policy change? In the nineteenth century, a number of groups formed with the aim of helping both mothers and children confront the health and education issues of the day. The General Federation of Women's Clubs (GFWC) was started in 1890 under the direction of Jane Cunningham Croly; it began as a network of local women's groups, then became an association of state federations. While at first the organization attracted mostly white middle-class women into its ranks, as it evolved, working-class women became involved as well; tragically, as a result of racism, African Americans were largely excluded.[24] While the organization worked on issues unrelated to motherhood, such as supporting American troops in wartime, it also engaged in multiple activities that directly benefited children. For example, it became deeply involved in the creation of public libraries across the United States as well as in the development of kindergartens. Also on its radar were the issues of child labor and health. With the assistance of Jane Addams, the organization helped create a Child Labor Committee to improve the safety of child workers. By 1916, more than two thousand clubs had joined together to confront the problems of infant and maternal mortality.[25] Their activism ultimately helped produce the 1921 Sheppard-Towner Act, which mandated federal funding for child and maternal health.

Because African American women were prohibited from joining the GFWC, they started their own organizations to deal with issues affecting their communities.[26] Two critical African American leaders—Josephine Ruffin and Mary Church Terrell—started the National Association of Colored Women's Clubs (NACWC) in 1896. During its initial years of operation, the group largely focused on campaigns around women's suffrage, as well as protests against lynching and Jim Crow laws. However, over time, the NACWC, like the GFWC, also became involved in a classic mothers' issue: improving the quality of children's education.

At the end of the century, in 1897, under the leadership of Phoebe Apperson Hearst and Alice McLellan Birney, the National Congress of Mothers was founded, with a primary focus on improving children's education. Despite opposition from school administrators, its founders were committed to the idea that parents, and at the time particularly mothers, become involved in their children's intellectual development.

During this new era of progressive politics, the organization distinguished itself by lobbying for federal aid for elementary schools, enhanced teacher salaries, and the extension of juvenile courts.[27] Like the GFWC, it argued that kindergarten was critical and helped implement such programs across the country. It also helped create the United States Children's Bureau in 1912, now under the Department of Health and Human Services, which works on such issues as child labor, child abuse, general living conditions, child welfare, and infant mortality.[28] It officially became the Parent Teacher Association (PTA) in 1924.

Whereas these organizations focused on mothers' relationships to their children's health and education, another key mothers' organization that formed during this time dealt with the conditions under which mothers could and should have children at all. Margaret Sanger set up her first office in Brooklyn, New York, in 1916, providing birth control information to largely poor and immigrant women, and in 1921 founded the American Birth Control League.[29] Sanger effectively fought against the Comstock Laws, which since the 1870s had made it illegal to give out information about birth control. By 1942, the organization had become the Planned Parenthood Federation of America and later went on to provide such services as the testing for and treatment of sexually transmitted infections, sexuality education, pregnancy testing, breast cancer screening, abortion services, and general reproductive health counseling.

Around the mid-twentieth century, a series of mothers' groups emerged that advocated for the ability of all women to provide for their children economically. The National Welfare Rights Organization, begun in 1966 under George Wiley, was typical of these groups.[30] Its mission centered on helping single-parent families, many of whom were African American and receiving welfare benefits. At this point in American social policy history, conservatives were increasingly arguing against spending more money on welfare programs. To counter these efforts, local churches and other organizations attempted to voice the needs and concerns of their communities, but individually, they were unable to make an impact on the tide of antiwelfare sentiment that was then sweeping the country. To address this problem more uniformly, the National Welfare Rights Organization pooled these voices into its one central mouthpiece to fight for such desired outcomes as adequate income, dignity, justice, and the right to democratic participation for welfare recipients.[31] Its central goal was to influence the debate on welfare reform proposals then being addressed in Congress, and the group made protecting livable benefit levels in the Aid to Families with Dependent Children (AFDC) program and the defeat of Nixon's proposed Family Assistance Plan (with low minimum-benefit levels) a priority. They continued their work apace before disbanding in 1975.

There were also the stirrings of attempts to redefine nutritional practices as they related to breastfeeding. La Leche League began in Chicago in 1956, under the primary tutelage of Mary White and Marian Thompson, to help promote breastfeeding among the general population. This was quite a radical idea at the time, since bottle feeding was becoming increasingly popular across American society.[32] Breastfeeding was also a countercultural idea in that women were moving from the home and into the workforce, giving them fewer opportunities to nourish their infants in this way. However, members of the league believed in the value of what they were promoting and maneuvered to turn conventional wisdom on its head regarding what a modern workplace should look like. The league argued that workplaces should accommodate breastfeeding by providing private mother-baby spaces and promoted the use of the electrical breast pump for times when mothers could not directly feed their infants. Their ideas made slow but steady inroads among mothers most interested in integrating modern workplaces with novel breastfeeding practices.

A last set of mothers' organizations formed in the later part of the twentieth century to protect their members' children from physical harm. Candy Lightner and Cindi Lamb began Mothers Against Drunk Driving (MADD) on September 5, 1980. Both women were personally affected by drunk drivers: Lightner's daughter had lost her life and Lamb's daughter had become paralyzed as a result of accidents involving the other driver's excessive use of alcohol.[33] MADD became an extremely important organization in American political life because it brought a completely unique perspective to the issue of drunk driving. Prior to its establishment, the media had focused on the cold statistics of alcohol-related injuries and deaths on the road, and car makers had directed their energies toward improving safety in vehicle construction rather than educating drivers on the importance of not drinking while driving. MADD was different; it gave a human face to the problem of drunk driving. Among its many accomplishments, MADD assisted in the enactment of stricter state laws against drunk driving, helped establish the new federal drinking age of twenty-one, and advocated for lower blood alcohol levels in defining legal inebriation.[34]

In another initiative to protect children from physical harm, the Million Mom March began as a rally held on Mother's Day, May 14, 2000. Donna Dees-Thomases, a New Jersey mother, had become increasingly horrified by the random gun violence occurring across the United States, especially violence directed at children. Along with several dozen other mothers, she applied for a permit to hold a march on the Washington Mall to protest what she felt was a lack of effective gun laws in the United States. The march attracted approximately 750,000 people, with an additional 150,000–200,000 marching in other locations across the country.[35] This initial rally later transformed into an organization with seventy-five local chapters; these work directly with the Brady Campaign to End Gun Violence, a well-respected nonprofit that raises awareness about gun violence in its various manifestations.

The Working World, a Mother's Place, and Modern Mothers' Organizations

Historical mothers' groups, as well as the five modern, national mothers' groups at the center of analysis here, all share the same fundamental goal: making the lives of their members and of their children more meaningful. While not always successful in achieving all their objectives, the historical organizations generally laid out clear public policy goals that attracted the passion of their members. This is true also of the five modern groups studied here; they all in some way have identifiable positions related to one key issue: promoting workplace flexibility. These five groups were thus chosen for study because of this overlapping issue of interest, but also because they are the only national groups that have members across multiple states and maintain centralized lists of their memberships, which is vital to the research design employed here.[36] But because of the many other roles that these groups play and the multiple issues on which they focus their attention, it is not clear where their members themselves stand on the advancement of workplace flexibility initiatives. Is there unity between these groups' public positions and their members' views, or divergence? Can a mothers' movement be built across all the groups, with workplace flexibility taking center stage? After all, constructing a mothers' movement in the twenty-first century over such a large population certainly can seem like a gargantuan task.[37]

In many ways, the origins of these five modern mothers' groups are fascinating. They were propelled into existence as a result of the massive upheaval in women's labor force participation that has occurred over the past fifty years. More specifically, the number of married women with children under eighteen in the American paid labor force skyrocketed during this period. In 1960, only 27.6 percent of these women were engaged in paid employment. By 1980, that number had grown to 54.1 percent and by 2010 had reached 71.3 percent.[38] The reasons behind these changes were numerous. Women were having smaller families, enabling them to focus on external interests. At the same time, men's real wages were falling, and mothers entered the paid labor market in financially supporting their families, to maintain their standard of living. Finally, the women's movement opened up educational opportunities for mothers and encouraged them to find self-satisfaction through paid employment. As a result of all these factors, mothers became a permanent fixture in the contemporary American workforce.

The road to paid work, however, was rocky.[39] Women struggled with the decision of how best to combine paid work (if at all) and unpaid work on a variety of fronts.[40] To cope with the diversity of these work-family challenges, mothers began turning to one another and joining organizations with various approaches to the topic of workplace flexibility. On one end of the spectrum is Mothers of Preschoolers (MOPS). Established in 1973, it stresses Christian values among its membership and participating local chapters must adhere to its religious doctrines. The majority of its approximately eighty-five thousand members stay at home; however, it encourages women who both stay at home and work for pay to join.[41] While it has no explicit policy on workplace flexibility, it does encourage personal fulfillment among all its members, and this may include these mothers putting together effective plans to engage in paid work.

In the middle of the organizational spectrum are Mocha Moms, Mothers & More, and the National Association of Mothers' Centers (NAMC), each of which has approximately 50 percent of its members working for pay. Mocha Moms began in 1997 and has about twenty-eight hundred members. While Mocha Moms has a concrete mission to serve at-home mothers of color, because many of its members want to work for pay at least on a part-time basis, the organization actively helps them establish flexible, at-home businesses. Mothers & More, with a membership of about fifty-three hundred, began in 1987 initially as an organization to help mothers transitioning in and out of the workforce, depending on their children's ages. It currently has a three-pronged advocacy and education statement in place called the Power Plan; one component of this plan is a fight for the ability of mothers to combine paid work with caretaking—including using workplace flexibility policies—if they so choose. NAMC started out in 1975 with a social work orientation and the goal of assisting mothers going through challenges with newborns. It later added a workforce advocacy component to its mission, embodied by its Mothers' Declaration of Rights, which states that mothers should be able to be caregivers as well as paid workers if they so desire. Inherent in this principle is that mothers be afforded flexible work opportunities. NAMC sponsors numerous work-life programs, such as conferences and blogs for its approximately nine hundred members.

At the opposite end of the spectrum from MOPS is MomsRising, an online group that expressly advocates for mothers working for pay. Formed in 2006, it has 169,000 members, the majority of whom are employed. Its primary advocacy mission is focused on improving the lives of mothers, around which workplace flexibility issues are central.

Along with the fact that these groups have different explicit perspectives on the issue of workplace flexibility is a real question of how much their positions are reflective of their members' actual belief systems and whether or not these belief systems can be mobilized into political action. For instance, how do each group's members view the concept of workplace flexibility overall? Do the members believe that it is relevant to their lives as mothers, or do only mothers who are currently working for pay have strong opinions about it? Do members of some groups tend to support all types of governmental workplace flexibility initiatives, such as tax breaks, educational efforts, and mandates on firms that implement such policies, while members of other groups tend to reject them? Are there major differences within groups, across groups, or again, depending on members' paid work status on these reform proposals? Considering the answers to all these questions together, are these mothers' group members more unified than divided on the issue of workplace flexibility, thus enabling them to build bridges in their approaches to solving problems facing the majority of mothers today? If so, then there are many as of yet untapped opportunities to promote intergroup mobilization and unite mothers definitively for the long term.

Research Methodology and Plan of the Book

Despite their importance in helping us understand the workplace and caregiving challenges that American mothers face in contemporary life, these five organizations simply have not had the resources to undertake a large-scale research project related to the attitudes, opinions, and behaviors of their membership bases.[42] In this book I seek to fill this knowledge vacuum through the use of three distinct research methodologies.

First, the analysis involved a random sample web-based survey of each group's membership in the spring of 2009 (final total sample size: 3,327); to generate comparative sociodemographic data, the study also included a phone-based random sample survey of eight hundred nongroup mothers during the same time period. To qualify for the phone survey, each respondent had to be at least eighteen years of age, have responsibility for at least one child age seventeen or under living in the home, and could not be a member of any of the five mothers' groups participating in the web survey. The random sampling design involved in each survey ensures that statements can be made about group mothers or nongroup mothers within a range of certainty. For example, if the surveys state that x percent of mothers involved in one group report being Hispanic, then it is also true that within a certain degree of certainty x percent of the entire group's population is Hispanic.

Second, during the period 2008–9, 125 in-depth interviews (25 per group) were conducted with members involved in these groups, to provide the survey data with richness and depth. These interviews offer the most important source of contextual material for the book in their portrayal of mothers struggling with work-family balance, a struggle that the survey data can outline only in numerical form.[43]

Third, each group was observed during one of its meetings and notes were taken on the proceedings (for MomsRising, the online group, there was a moderated, structured online chat) in 2008–9. This triangulation of methods—surveys, interviews, and observation—strengthened the reliability and validity of the findings generated here. Further description of the survey methodology, as well as a list of the in-depth interview questions, are found elsewhere in the appendix.

The plan of the book is as follows. In chapter 2 I provide a more detailed history of the five organizations included in this study, describing their origins, development, and current missions. I pay particular attention to the position each organization has on workplace flexibility and the implications of the position for its members. I then use the nationally representative survey data to present a portrait of exactly who is joining mothers' groups today. I examine the sociodemographic profile of mothers who are currently members of these groups across the country, thereby providing a sense of what types of women are looking for support in the form of an organizational community of parents. In the chapter I also present sociodemographic data on the mothers who participated in the in-depth interviews.

In chapter 3 I then explore exactly *why* women have been motivated to join these special groups that serve mothers with varying degrees of attachment to the paid labor force. Throughout their children's development from infancy through adolescence, many mothers find that they need interpersonal support. Yet with current patterns of residential life that frequently spread families and friends widely apart geographically, mothers need to find their own methods of coping with the stresses of everyday parenthood.[44] For women in the paid workforce, their place of employment may not be ideal for discussing the difficulties they face in their personal lives.[45] They may feel anxious over proving to their supervisors and co-workers that they are serious workers and not overly distracted by family problems. They also might want to keep their family life issues to themselves. Of course, stay-at-home mothers might have even fewer opportunities to meet with and obtain support from other women experiencing parenting and other types of familial challenges. In this chapter I thus analyze mothers' groups for their ability to provide a whole host of resources to women, including day-to-day assistance with parenting information and forums to better manage their work-family balance conundrums.

In chapter 4 I discuss whether the reportedly deeply held divisions between stay-at-home mothers and mothers who work for pay actually exist. The media has repeatedly highlighted such divisions under the label "the Mommy Wars." Indeed, from morning and daytime television to popular books and advice gurus, is seems that no one can escape the sharp force of the weaponry generated by these wars. With the issue's saturation coverage, this chapter importantly notes that in the majority of cases, mothers are *not* judgmental of one another. Instead, they empathize with each mother's unique situation. Despite this common ground, this chapter does reveal that in a minority of cases, stereotypes of each group still exist, thus making mutual understanding a top priority of any modern motherhood movement.

While chapter 4 draws attention to the commonalities and only the small number of differences that drive mothers apart, in chapter 5 I delve into workplace flexibility as a unifying concept for bringing all mothers together. I explore across groups and the work-for-pay/stay-at-home divide the question of whether mothers tend to support various workplace flexibility initiatives. In addition, I explore the levels of support that exist for governmental policies promoting workplace flexibility, ranging from educating firms about the benefits of such options, to tax breaks for companies that offer such plans, to mandatory requirements that organizations offer employees processes through which to request and even receive such arrangements. In doing so, I offer possible parameters for policy makers to think about as they design reforms to generate the widest levels of public support.

In chapter 6 I ask the direct question of whether the mothers who are participating in these groups now believe that they are participating in some type of mothers' movement through their organizational affiliation on the issue of workplace flexibility. The chapter then moves on to the question of whether workplace flexibility can provide a foundation for such a movement in the future. As the book will have demonstrated up until this point, the research behind workplace flexibility in terms of helping workers, and in particular mothers, manage their work and family lives is quite substantial. In addition, the organizational infrastructure to help effect change on the political level has already been established by these groups. What additional measures are necessary, then, to articulate flexibility as the critical workplace goal to be achieved in this new century?

In chapter 7 I directly consider the concrete steps that must be taken for workplace flexibility to become a viable part of the American employment structure. First, I examine the leadership that is essential in the world of public policy, such as lawmakers' educating the public and promoting incentives for businesses to become more engaged on this topic. I also explore the role of legal mandates in promoting change in the current political climate. Second, I focus on the leadership that must come from the groups that are spotlighted in this study. I point out the ways in which these groups could become more vested in the clear workplace flexibility desires of their members, which could ultimately harbinger the changes a unified mothers' movement could dramatically bring to fruition across the nation.

2

Power in Numbers

The scene is a Roman Catholic Church basement in a large city on the East Coast. While there is only a little natural light breaking into the room through the small windows, the space is brightened by both the blue tile floor and the mood of the participants. There are twelve African American mothers from the group Mocha Moms enjoying snacks in a circle. Their children are seated at an adjacent table. It is a cold weekend morning right after the 2008 presidential election and the kids are happily coloring Barack Obama pictures. In the midst of this joyous celebration, the chapter president calls the group to order. The members then begin a lively discussion about the implications of this presidential election on their group's future agenda.

MOCHA MOMS PRESIDENT: Yes, we did! (referring to Obama victory). Where was everyone when you heard the news that Obama won?

MOCHA MOMS MEMBER 1: Was anyone worried that he wouldn't win? . . .

MOCHA MOMS MEMBER 2: I started crying because my daughter gets to see people like me in that office. I want to create change, too.

MOCHA MOMS MEMBER 1: Obama inspires people. The prayer and hope is that he is able to make change.

MOCHA MOMS MEMBER 3: My mother-in-law grew up in the segregated South and she still watches political shows. The older folks can't believe it . . .

MOCHA MOMS MEMBER 4: I bought a book for my six-year-old girl about Obama. In the book, it talks about him waking up early to do his homework.

MOCHA MOMS MEMBER 2: How do we [take advantage of this change and] affect what happens outside this group?

In November 2008, these Mocha Moms members were clearly excited. Barack Obama had just been elected president, and they viewed this as a teachable moment for their children and their communities. Most important, they wanted to harness the momentum of the event to produce positive outcomes for their group chapters and beyond. But clearly this group was not starting from zero in terms of resources. There was decisive energy in the room and a strong sense of sisterhood among its members. This was a group with a vibrant and engaged history.

How did mothers' organizations like Mocha Moms—specifically MOPS, Mothers & More, NAMC, and MomsRising—come into being in the associational landscape? How have the groups changed over time, in both scope and mission? What does each group's membership look like now, specifically with respect to its sociodemographic characteristics?

While mothers' groups have clearly emerged from the changing economic landscape of the past several decades, in each case, it took the initiative of one or a small set of leaders to begin a conversation about how they wanted their lives to be transformed through a new organizational community. Notably, these emergent leaders were each in a variety of circumstances, from working for pay, to transitioning into or out from the workforce, to staying at home. Nonetheless, across all five groups, the leaders perceived a sense of dissatisfaction, stress, and feeling of disenchantment with their lives as mothers. They therefore sought out mothers like themselves to find support and fulfill other needs that were so important to them at the time through an innovative group format. These are their stories.

Prayer and Motherhood: MOPS

MOPS (Mothers of Preschoolers) is a Christian-based organization of chapters that focuses on the needs of mothers with preschoolers.[1] While it does not have an explicit position on workplace flexibility, it welcomes both stay-at-home mothers and mothers who work for pay and encourages both groups to reach their full potential. Its website frequently presents articles on the challenges facing mothers who work for pay, including those mothers who wish to resolve these issues by establishing more flexible, at-home businesses. In terms of its meeting style, ideally, national MOPS asks that each local session include four components: social (food and fellowship), teaching from a biblical perspective, small-group discussion, and creative time. While attending meetings, MOPS members drop their children off at MOPPETS, a child care program oriented toward their developmental stage. The central goal behind the MOPS organization is to equip mothers to meet their own needs so they can ultimately make the world a better place. To fulfill this mission, MOPS aims to instill in its members qualities that will ultimately help them assume leadership positions outside the boundaries of the organization.

The organization began in 1973, when Maxine Shideler read a magazine article that described the challenges women faced in raising toddlers in the United States. Fascinated by this piece, she brought together seven other women to form MOPS in Wheat Ridge, Colorado. They met in a children's playroom at the Trinity Baptist Church, sitting together on tiny chairs made for their children. At this initial meeting, the women enjoyed each other's friendship and discussed their vision for the group. They wanted to create a safe space to be themselves as they faced the ups and downs of motherhood, and they knew immediately that they wanted their group to have a strong biblical dimension. At the core of their emerging belief system was the idea that mothering was a critical societal practice that until then had not been properly acknowledged or appreciated. They integrated discussion, religion, and craftwork as a way to build community and a sense of accomplishment among the core set of women who participated. They also believed that they could learn from each other as parents, and they asked fellow mother Naomi Michie to be the group's teaching leader. Once she agreed, Michie led thirty-minute instructional sessions on issues of importance to the women, and enabling feelings of security and self-esteem became paramount. From these initial meetings, the organization grew, and in 1981, it established a board of directors and incorporated as MOPS Outreach and later as MOPS Inc.

From this starting point, the number of groups ticked upward to approximately sixty by the early 1980s. Growth really exploded after Dr. James Dobson from Focus on the Family, an international Christian ministry group emphasizing family values, provided MOPS with an opportunity to describe its mission on his radio show. By the late 1980s as a result of publicity such as this, the number of MOPS chapters skyrocketed to over four hundred. By 1988, the group had established a presence abroad and changed its name to MOPS International. At this point, the board of directors realized that it could no longer rely on a team of volunteers to guide the group into the future; bursting at the seams, MOPS needed a more formal, paid staff. In 1989 the organization hired Elisa Morgan as its president.

Communication was key to its early success. In 1993 MOPS established a newsletter and then a magazine called *MomSense*, which was quickly followed by a radio show of the same name. The organization entered into a partnership with the Zondervan Publishing House in 1995 and formed a collaboration with Revell of the Baker Publishing Group in 2004. Both these initiatives were designed to keep the organization connected to companies that could enlarge the organization's outreach efforts to mothers across the globe. Finally, also of note during this time was the creation of Teen MOPS for adolescent mothers in 1995 and, in 1997, the introduction of an online presence for interested mothers.

As a Christian organization, according to its website, "MOPS International exists to encourage, equip and develop every mother of preschoolers to realize her potential as a woman, mother and leader in the name of Jesus Christ." There are numerous organizational principles that guide MOPS chapters. Although nondenominational, all MOPS chapters must affiliate with a local church or parachurch group, respect the heritage of the group, and practice good governance. All MOPS groups must also establish strong alliances with other institutions that could be helpful in achieving its goals. Last, all groups must adhere to MOPS' International Faith Position Statement, which outlines the group's beliefs as they relate to Jesus Christ.

MOPS also has what it calls six ministry values that it aims to have permeate all its work. These emphasize (1) respecting the dignity of all human life; (2) equipping women to be all they can be; (3) valuing mothers and their contributions; (4) fostering all adult and parent-child relationships, as well as a relationship with Jesus Christ; (5) engaging in "lifestyle evangelism," whereby members are encouraged to bring others toward Jesus Christ through their daily choices, rather than overt preaching; and (6) fostering leadership development for women.

All Mothers Are Not White: Mocha Moms

Mocha Moms engages in the workplace flexibility policy arena by providing, as part of its national platform, particular entrepreneurial support for mothers with their own at-home businesses.[2] In addition, it devotes resources to maintaining two national networks of mothers. Networks are simply subgroups within Mocha Moms that are dedicated to specific issue areas. These networks are connected via the Internet and promote the sharing of writing, personal stories, and advice. Mochas in Transition, the first network, offers services to any member experiencing caregiving or employment changes; Work at Home, the second network, does the same for mothers who either work at home for an employer or have their own home-based business.

The group began organically, when several stay-at-home mothers of color wanted to reach out to similar mothers located across the country. Cheli English-Figaro, an African American attorney, was married to a military physician when the air force relocated them to Bowie, Maryland, in 1992. English-Figaro found herself very isolated when she decided to leave paid employment to be a full-time mother to her newborn son in 1993. She had not planned to stay at home, and very few of her African American friends or family members understood why she would abandon her career to remain at home. In the fall of 1993, she joined the Officers' Wives Club, where she found only one other mother of color in similar circumstances. Still seeking companionship, she started attending meetings at La Leche League and continued networking with other groups such as Lawyers at Home and the Landover Memorial Baptist Church Mothers' Group (the church is now Woodstream Church). Although she did not find complete satisfaction in these other groups, her efforts at forging new relationships paid off in July 1994, when her son had his first birthday. With about thirty stay-at-home mothers of color over at her townhouse to celebrate, she used the opportunity to present her vision for a long-term supportive community that she wanted to begin as soon as possible. The foundation of the group was officially laid.

Three years later, in Cheverly, Maryland, two other African American women were experiencing the same need to connect with other mothers of color who were staying at home with their children. Jolene Ivey and Karla Chutz (the wife of an air force officer), considering the advice of a friend, Dia Michels (a white stay-at-home mother), decided that the best way to link up with other African American stay-at-home mothers was through the production of a mother-oriented newsletter, which came to be called *Mocha Moms*. Through mutual friends, English-Figaro heard about this innovative newsletter and reached out to Ivey directly. English-Figaro introduced Ivey to her own group of stay-at-home mothers of color at a local McDonalds during the summer of 1997. Two weeks after this initial get-together, the new friends decided to move beyond the newsletter to form a new organization of like-minded stay-at-home mothers of color. At this first meeting at Ivey's home, English-Figaro was joined by Ivey, Chutz, Pauletta Handy (a friend of English-Figaro from the Landover Church mothers' group), and Nikki Haynes, a Muslim stay-at-home mother who had learned about the group through the *Mocha Moms* newsletter. Handy expressed a strong preference that the group have a Christian orientation; however, English-Figaro, Ivey, Chutz, and Haynes did not necessarily want to exclude mothers of other faiths. In the end, the majority decided that the group should remain secular. After this decision, Handy dropped out of the nascent organization, but soon another enthusiastic mother, Joby Dupree, took her place. A military wife herself, Dupree immediately discovered that she had a lot in common with English-Figaro and Chutz.

With these five women at its core, Mocha Moms started to grow and eventually became an incorporated organization. The mothers planned the organization and its activities at Ivey's house, at her church, and later, in local playgrounds. Jill Downing became another central player in the organization, helping English-Figaro develop a handbook that they hoped new groups would use in starting their own local chapters. English-Figaro and Downing later traveled all over the country to spread the word about their group. They hoped that, through the valuable connections engendered by Mocha Moms, mothers of color would no longer feel isolated when they stayed home with their children.

The current mission of Mocha Moms is to support women of color who have chosen not to work full time outside the home at the current stage in their lives. However, many of Mocha Moms' members still participate in the paid labor market in some capacity, by working from home, running their own business, or participating in some type of part-time employment. In addition to its efforts in assisting mothers in all these circumstances, Mocha Moms has other core principles that make up its platform: nonexclusivity, support for community activism, nonpartisanship, advocacy of married relationships, self-care, and the education of its members' children.

Mocha Moms' organizational structure consists of its National Executive Board, as well as its National Advisory Council, which offers the board guidance on important topics facing the group. In addition, Mocha Moms has regional directors and state coordinators who can pool the resources of local chapters in pursuing common projects. Each local chapter, however, is responsible for electing its own leaders and running its organization on its own. The chapters are charged with holding monthly or bimonthly meetings, as well as participating in two community service projects a year. Finally, local chapters must plan mothers-only events in order to give women the opportunity to socialize with others without having to supervise their children at the same time.

Politics through the Backdoor: Mothers & More

Mothers & More has an explicit, well-developed position on workplace flexibility.[3] Three core beliefs guide its actions on this front: (1) all the work that mothers do, whether paid or unpaid, has social and economic value; (2) mothers should be able to fulfill their caregiving responsibilities without social and economic penalties; (3) all women should have support for their right to choose if and how to combine parenting and paid employment, which includes having access to workplace flexibility policies. In pursuing these goals, Mothers & More actively endorses educational efforts among its members about these important issues, but also works with state and local governments to make sure that public policy adequately addresses mothers' needs.

This organization started when Joanne Brundage, a letter carrier from Elmhurst, Illinois, decided to leave her job after the birth of her second child. She never imagined she would have such mixed emotions about her decision. She knew that her baby son needed extra attention, yet she missed the purpose, camaraderie, and self-sufficiency that she had enjoyed at her paid job. When she described her conflict to her smaller group of friends and acquaintances, however, she sensed that they could not relate to her frustrations. To counter this, on August 5, 1987, she placed an advertisement in her local newspaper asking other stay-at-home mothers to join her in the creation of a group that would cater to their unique needs by providing support to one another.

This first group of mothers met in Brundage's home about a week later, on August 13, and was originally called F.E.M.A.L.E., or Formerly Employed Mothers at Loose Ends. Brundage explicitly wanted the group not to be a simple parenting community, but rather an organization where mothers could recognize, simply through the name of the group, what its composition and goals would be. Although the initial meeting attracted only four members, besides Brundage, by the end of the year, over fifteen mothers were regularly attending. Three of the four original members ended up serving on the board that formed that year.

During the first meetings in 1987, the members decided that they wanted to cast the widest possible net for interested moms to participate in the group. In October, the organization placed ads in the *Chicago Tribune*'s weekly WomanNews section under "Support Groups." Intrigued by the notices, a *Tribune* reporter wrote a small accompanying story about the group on page 2 of WomanNews in the paper's December 20, 1987, edition. Within two days of the ad's appearing, Brundage received sixty-four calls. She immediately had to find a space that could accommodate the expected surge in attending mothers and ultimately filled a classroom at a local junior high school to capacity at the organization's meeting on January 5, 1988. The group received more attention when *Ms. Magazine* published a letter by Brundage in March that year in response to the magazine's coverage of a similar, Canadian stay-at-home mothers' group.

Here in suburban Chicago a number of us have recently formed a group, Formerly Employed Mothers at Loose Ends (F.E.M.A.L.E.). . . . We are mothers who spent a number of years in the paid workforce, intend to return to that workforce sooner or later, but in the meantime are taking time out to care for our young children.

Whatever the individual circumstances that led to our quitting paid employment, we share many of the same difficulties making this transition: a loss of identity, self-esteem, direction, and structure; envy and/or condescension from family, friends, and former coworkers; redefining our roles in our familial and marital relationships and relinquishing the security and pleasures of financial autonomy.[4]

This letter, and coverage from several other major national newspapers in 1988, provoked correspondence from women all over the country who wanted to start their own local chapters of the organization. In the *Washington Post* on May 31, 1988, Brundage was profiled as a pioneer, one who acknowledged, "I had never realized that my job was so integral to my feelings about myself. It's a given a man is what he's done. But women have not been consciously defined that way. When you quit, you find that's true for women, too."[5] Brundage hoped her group would help women in similar circumstances. Using organizational materials from La Leche League as a guide for its development, the organization started building chapters all over the country by 1989.

In these early years, Brundage and others at the top of the organization used the term *sequencing* to describe mothers moving out of the paid labor force temporarily to raise their children. Featuring this term in her book *Sequencing*, on which F.E.M.A.L.E. drew, Arlene Rossen Cardozo championed this model of "in the paid labor market—out of the paid labor market while children are young—in the paid labor market again when children get older" as the best way for women to cope with the demands of their jobs and their caregiving needs.[6] Initially when women inquired about membership in F.E.M.A.L.E., they received a newsletter and book recommendations from the organization. These recommendations included not only *Sequencing*, but also *Staying Home Instead* by Christine Davidson and *A Mother's Work* by Deborah Fallows, each of which advocated for a period when mothers could stay at home and spend time with their children before returning to paid work.[7]

As the chapters grew in both size and number, the organization changed its name to Formerly Employed Mothers at the Leading Edge in May 1991. This name change was enacted primarily for strategic reasons.[8] The organization was attempting to hold on to members who were "aging out" of the original chapters by, most commonly, returning to paid work. The new name would thus reflect the organization's efforts to retain them by declaring that they were no longer at "loose ends" but were at the "leading edge" of moving their families productively into the future. In addition, the organization wanted to appeal to all mothers, not just sequencing mothers. The leadership truly desired that stay-at-home mothers, mothers working in the paid labor market, and sequencing mothers all feel comfortable within the group. But the debate over the group's name did not end there, and on June 1, 2000, the organization underwent its third and last name change when it became Mothers & More. This final change was intended to demonstrate that mothers are multifaceted and that the distinction between working moms and stay-at-home moms is artificial, with most mothers moving in and out of paid employment over their life course. The new name also had appeal in that it was shorter and thus hopefully easier to remember for prospective recruits.

Currently, the organization defines itself as being dedicated to improving the lives of mothers through support, education, and advocacy. Much of the group's activities take place at the local chapters in the form of regular meetings held at night—without children present. Chapters are directed toward mothers' needs and interests as individual women, and toward promoting discussion, special interest groups, and joint decision making in how the groups are run. In addition, chapters typically hold adult-only Moms' Night Out activities for recreational purposes and daytime playgroups where members can get together with their children. The organization encourages its local chapters to raise community awareness of key social and economic issues affecting mothers through, for example, its annual Mother's Day Campaign, whose focus varies from year to year. While these events are central to the organization's mission, Mothers & More is also active online. The organization has over twenty e-mail discussion groups, offers periodic public and member-only surveys, and in other ways explores the dilemmas facing the modern mother through its website, mothersandmore.org.

The group currently has eight core principles that guide its operation, as detailed on its website:

1. A mother is more than any single role she plays at any given point in her lifetime. She is entitled to fully explore and develop her identity as she chooses: as a woman, a citizen, a parent or an employee.
2. All the work mothers do—whether paid or unpaid—has social and economic value.
3. Caregiving work is real work with real social and economic value.
4. All women deserve recognition and support for their right to choose if and how to combine parenting and paid employment.
5. All mothers, all children and all families are unique. We respect the wisdom of each mother to decide how to care for her children, her family and herself.
6. Mothers have the right to fulfill their caregiving responsibilities without incurring social and economic penalties.
7. The transitions women make into and through motherhood are challenging and can be difficult.
8. Together, mothers are powerful.

Taking Care of Daily Needs:
National Association of Mothers' Centers

NAMC (National Association of Mothers' Centers) also actively works on behalf of workplace flexibility issues.[9] It does this directly by sponsoring an annual work-life conference for employees and employers searching to improve their flexibility options; promoting annual awards in workplace excellence in the area of flexibility, in conjunction with the Alfred P. Sloan Foundation; and providing Internet resources for mothers looking for workplace support. A further effort toward this goal is its MOTHERS (Mothers Ought to Have Equal Rights) initiative. This is a netroots mobilization campaign to educate mothers, caregivers, and others about the importance of caregiving and how workplaces might be transformed to benefit all workers with enhanced flexibility across the board. The initiative explores how public policy affects mothers and families and how members can communicate with their legislators to advocate on behalf of workplace flexibility.

NAMC began in the early 1970s, when social worker Patsy Turrini was working in Nassau County, New York. While providing services to the community, Turrini came into contact with many mothers who were suffering from diminished confidence and related low self-esteem. After observing these mothers' problems, Turrini decided to enroll all interested individuals into a research study where they would come together to discuss areas of common concern. Initially, forty mothers volunteered to participate. With these mothers as her core members, Turrini based the format of the research sessions on early women's health initiative groups that were designed to facilitate information exchanges and included a focus on psychoanalytic principles. Turrini adapted this model for her participants—her sessions were premised on person-to-person advocacy, nonjudgmental discussion, decentralized communication, and nonhierarchical teaching and learning.

After the study ended, seventeen of the original forty women resolved to continue meeting to pursue the model's therapeutic effects and possibly help replicate it for other mothers. Turrini joined forces with Lorri Slepian, a peer social worker from the Women's Liberation Center and a research group facilitator. With seventeen interested women, they all established the first Mothers' Center, called the Family Service Association of Nassau County in Hicksville, New York. Interestingly, there was some discussion at the beginning about whether it should be a parent center; however, the group decided early on to focus its efforts on empowering solely women and mothers. News of the group soon spread like wildfire, and group leaders at the Hicksville location began fielding calls from mothers all over the country asking how they could start their own centers. To meet this demand, the Family Service Association of Nassau County began the Mothers' Center Development Project in 1981, with Slepian as the principal project director and Marge Milch as codirector. Following coverage of the mothers' center model on the *Phil Donahue Show* and an article in *Parents* magazine in 1984, the organization received over ten thousand inquiries from women all over the country who wanted to join.

With this overwhelming response, the Mothers' Center Development Project was incorporated as a separate 501(c)(3) organization under the name National Association of Mothers' Centers (NAMC) in 1993, with the aim of developing chapters all over the United States. Slepian and Linda Landsman, a founder of another local Mothers' Center, became the codirectors. NAMC's first overall goal was to provide a space in which women could come together to speak freely about the issues that they face as parents, whether these involve direct caregiving concerns such as child development and parenting techniques, or stress over work-family balance. With regular participation, mothers could gain increased self-confidence so they could move forward and advocate for themselves as citizens, parents, and workers. In sum, with these unified efforts, NAMC sought to elevate the work of motherhood and create a solid foundation for a society dedicated to these women's needs and interests.

NAMC engaged in several experimental enterprises in order to continue to increase the number of chapters with this philosophy in mind. First, the organization joined forces with the Young Women's Christian Association (YWCA) to establish Mothers' Centers across the latter's already established facilities. However, after a period of working with NAMC on the project, the YWCA decided to cease direct services of this type, and the partnership ended. Later, NAMC began working with Family Place Libraries to establish new groups in local libraries with many mothers and young children. This project continues to this day.

At the turn of the century, NAMC started to move in a more political direction. This is not to say that the organization had never taken on issues debated in the public arena. In fact, in its early years of development, NAMC had helped promote change on the ground by championing sibling visitation in hospitals after mothers gave birth, advancing the groundbreaking idea that stores and restaurants should be stroller friendly, and producing booklets that compiled members' preferences on local obstetricians and pediatricians, among other resources. In 1999, the national NAMC Board of Trustees went even further by announcing its support of the Million Mom March, a pro–gun control event in Washington, DC, and encouraged its chapters to take part.

In 2002, NAMC further pursued its policy-oriented goals on work-family life by drafting a Mothers' Declaration of Rights, which focused on the varied economic, social, educational, psychological, and physical needs of mothers across the country. In October that year, NAMC leaders, members, and volunteers met for a retreat at the Woodhull Institute in upstate New York. With the assistance of noted journalist Ann Crittenden, author of the highly acclaimed, pathbreaking book, *The Price of Motherhood*, the NAMC board and interested members established MOTHERS, described earlier, to focus on the economic consequences of caregiving.[10] Annual publicity events have included 2003's No More Zeroes campaign, to overturn the Social Security Administration's calculation that no benefits accrue for the years in which mothers are involved in unpaid carework, and the 2006 Ceasefire in the Mommy Wars campaign, designed to refute the media's characterization of working moms and stay-at-home moms being in constant philosophical opposition to one another. The organization ramped up its online presence by distributing regular e-newsletters and working on women-centered blogs. As part of this campaign, Valerie Young became the new advocacy coordinator, bringing work-family issues to light on Capitol Hill through her *DC Dispatch* column and *Your (Wo)Man in Washington* blog (wiw.mothercenter.org).

In-Your-Face Politics: MomsRising

MomsRising, too, has a strongly developed policy on workplace flexibility.[11] In its highly publicized M.O.T.H.E.R.S. campaign, each letter stands for a particular reform goal, many of which are part of its workplace flexibility agenda:

*M*aternity and paternity leave
*O*pen flexible work
*T*oxics-free homes
*H*ealthy kids
*E*xcellent child care
*R*ealistic and fair wages
*S*ick days (paid)

The organization attempts to influence public policy on these issues using techniques that include providing direct information to its members, encouraging its members to reach out to legislative leaders, aligning itself with approximately 150 like-minded organizations to work on common goals, and offering tools to employers to improve their work practices. As described earlier, MomsRising is unique among the groups studied here in that it is primarily an online organization. It communicates with its members who sign up on its website via regular blogs, its Facebook page, and Twitter messages.

The organization was founded after Joan Blades, the wildly successful entrepreneur and cofounder of Moveon.org, could not believe what she was reading as she casually glanced through a new book one day in 2004. She opened Kristen Rowe-Finkbeiner's *The F-Word: Feminism in Jeopardy* and learned that there still was a massive pay discrepancy between the sexes.[12] This discrepancy was even worse when the pay of men and mothers was compared. After giving this issue some thought, Blades wrote a two-page document that year called the "Mothers' Manifesto," which discussed this employment inequality problem. Much of her analysis was based on her belief that first, this was an important issue affecting all parents who want to both take care of their children and earn a living, and second, that the issue had the potential to cross party lines. This is the text that she circulated to close friends at the time:

"Motherhood Manifesto"—Supporting the Family, by Joan Blades

80% of women become mothers. Most women work. When you ask young women what they are personally concerned about, most are worried about how they are going to balance work and children. These women are right on point. Many have seen their mothers struggle to balance work and family. Most work is not parent friendly. Ask any mother who has a full-time job. (Yes, women do still shoulder the lion's share of the parenting and it is reflected in their compensation. Data show that women make less than men doing the same job. Childless women make 10% less, women with children make 29% less.) Working a 40 hour week, with commute time frankly does not leave primary care providers with adequate time to care. Women who return to full-time work after 3 months maternity leave weep. It is an unnatural act for a mother to leave a young baby for 9 to 10 hours a day unless that baby is left with a deeply trusted relative such as a grandmother, a luxury most mothers lack. Young children learn to be apart from their parents for long periods, but they crave more time with their parents. Mothers feel their child's longing for them and are torn by the need to work and their children's needs. And then children get sick. Mothers search for excellent child care with mixed success. Most child care providers are part of the working poor and hence there is frequent turnover and they are often under trained. . . . One might imagine that our society does not value children or parenting highly.

The above assumes a full-time job that is 40 hours a week. Now consider that upwardly mobile American workers often work 50, 60 and 70 hour weeks. (Ever wonder about the glass ceiling for women?) The U.S. is proud of its high productivity, but that high productivity is as much an outcome of the huge numbers of hours worked as efficiency. European workers have somewhere around twice the vacation days and vastly shorter work weeks. Now, considering that we need to create more jobs, this might be an opportunity for the U.S. to make our families stronger, our lives richer and the unemployment rate lower.

What drives companies to ask their workers to work longer and longer hours and avoid hiring more employees? Benefits appear to be a primary motivation. As health care costs have risen without restraint over the last decade benefits have become a heavy burden that challenge both individuals and corporations. How many strikes have been about benefits in the last ten years? What strike hasn't? Even outsourcing is in part attributable to the high cost of benefits in the U.S.

In fact we might find that the advantages of a national health care system substantially outweigh the costs. The downward spiral of care in emergency rooms endangers us all. The advantages of providing health care to children and adults early rather than delaying until a time of crisis are self evident. The cost of health care has risen to the point that the average American family spends more upon heath care than gas. (Remember how economists worry about high gas prices undermining the economy because consumers have less to spend?)

Our health care system is broken. Incremental change will not fix what ails us and frankly I don't want the insurance and pharmaceutical industry writing the recommendations for how to fix the health care system. They are understandably afraid to think outside the box. They are the entities benefiting from the current dysfunction. I want the doctors who studied medicine to help people and patients who need care, alongside economists and other strategic thinkers to formulate a solution that embraces the big picture. Envision a society that values mothers, children, and all workers, the way to achieve this vision is with a systems approach that recognizes the complex dynamics of the choices we make.

If our leaders take a strategic look at our society there is a coming together of issues and opportunities that is quite remarkable. Championing motherhood, children, job creation, job preservation and health care . . . Creating an environment in which we all have the best possible opportunity to thrive is a worthy task for policy makers, politicians and citizens alike . . . and it will only happen when we determine that we will do it together. We need to support leaders with vision and find a way to free them from the cacophony of special interest voices that create deadly riptides and sink holes that obstruct the path of progress. Some day we will publicly finance elections so that candidates need never worry about even the appearance of impropriety. In the meantime, because money is a powerful force, we must counter that power with personal engagement by the citizenry. Real person to person connections can counter the power of money.

This brief document eventually became the book *The Motherhood Manifesto*, cowritten by Blades and Kristin Rowe-Finkbeiner and published in 2006.[13] It was the impetus behind the beginning, on Mother's Day, 2006, of MomsRising.org.

MomsRising has a set of core issues, all of which focus on bringing the challenges of parenting and motherhood onto the national public agenda. Members primarily join on the Internet as individuals; however, there are a few experimental chapters that meet in person, along with occasional book and play groups that are planned at the local level. For the most part, though, group members meet up with one another electronically and drive campaigns to pressure policy makers into changing regulations and laws that directly affect families.

TABLE 2.1.
Age and total number of children: Aggregate survey and interview data

	All nongroup mothers	All group mothers	
		Survey	Interviews
Current age (years)	41.59	37.72	37.37
Total number of children	2.04	2.02	2.09
Total sample size	800	3,327	125

TABLE 2.2.
Age and total number of children: Survey and interview data by group

	NAMC		MomsRising		MOPS		Mocha Moms		Mothers & More	
	Survey	Interviews	Survey	Interviews	Survey	Interviews	Survey	Interviews	Survey	Interviews
Current age (years)	38.93	39.20	41.47	37.76	35.22	35.72	37.70	36.04	37.69	38.12
Total number of children	1.91	2.00	1.78	1.84	2.27	2.56	2.05	2.20	1.92	1.84
Total sample size	182	25	461	25	762	25	620	25	1302	25

Who Joins Mothers' Groups Today?

The founding stories of all these organizations are different, and they have distinctive approaches to the issue of workplace flexibility, but they all place mothers at the top of their priorities. When we consider who joins these groups, there are both marked similarities and differences among their members. What, then, do the women who join mothers' groups look like today?

Recall from chapter 1 that this study drew upon two random sample surveys—one of group members and one of nongroup members—in order to tell us about what mothers as a whole look like in these two populations. In contrast, statistics generated from the interview data shed light on only the 125 group mothers who participated in this one-hour dialogue. As tables 2.1 and 2.2 indicate, across the group and nongroup surveys and in the interview pool, on average, mothers had approximately two children under the age of eighteen. The mothers in groups were about thirty-seven years old, and nongroup mothers slightly older. As revealed by both the survey and interview data, MOPS members had the most children and were the youngest mothers in the study.

Over half, or 51.1 percent of all group members were engaged in paid work, according to the survey, which was slightly less than the percentage of all mothers working for pay who were not involved in mothers' groups (see tables 2.3 and 2.4). The 125 interview respondents were more likely to report working for pay, at 60 percent. In general, in both the survey and interviews, MOPS members were the least likely to be working for pay, while MomsRising members were the most likely to be working for pay.

Mothers involved in mothers' groups, according to both the survey and the interview data, were extremely well educated. As tables 2.5 and 2.6

TABLE 2.3.
Current paid work status: Aggregate survey and interview data (%)

	All nongroup mothers	All group mothers	
		Survey	Interviews
Yes	59.9	51.1	60
No	40.1	48.9	40

TABLE 2.4.
Current paid work status: Survey and interview data by group (%)

	NAMC		MomsRising		MOPS		Mocha Moms		Mothers & More	
	Survey	Interviews	Survey	Interviews	Survey	Interviews	Survey	Interviews	Survey	Interviews
Yes	52.7	68	73.8	84	34.4	44	51.8	68	52.3	36
No	47.3	32	26.2	16	65.6	56	48.2	32	47.7	64

indicate, in contrast to the nongroup mothers, almost all the group mothers surveyed and interviewed had obtained at least some college experience. Moreover, while only 15.7 percent of all nongroup mothers ever attained professional training or a graduate degree, 41.8 percent of group mothers surveyed and 48 percent of group mothers interviewed for this project had achieved such a high level of education. These patterns were repeated across groups, with only MOPS dropping to 21.4 percent in terms of obtaining professional training or a graduate degree among its surveyed members.

With respect to the group members' race and ethnicity, tables 2.7 and 2.8 provide a fairly straightforward picture. In terms of nongroup mothers, approximately three-fourths of the population are white, while about one in ten are black or Hispanic. When exploring group membership in both the surveys and interviews, however, while the number of whites stays the same, the number of blacks increases to one in five. However, the number of Hispanics in these groups tumbles to close to zero. The mystery behind these numbers is solved when we break out the membership by group. With the exception of Mocha Moms, the groups are overwhelmingly white. Mocha Moms, catering to the needs of women of color, adds racial diversity to the overall aggregate figures in that close to nine out of its ten members are black. In addition, as these figures demonstrate, white Hispanics, black Hispanics, Asian Americans, and Native Americans are attracted to these groups in very low numbers.

TABLE 2.5.
Education: Aggregate survey and interview data (%)

	All nongroup mothers	All group mothers	
		Survey	Interviews
Less than high school (grade 11 or less)	7.7	0	0
High school diploma (including GED)	17.9	1.1	0
Some college, but did not graduate	19.2	7.3	4.0
Associate's degree (two-year degree) or specialized technical	14.8	5.9	3.2
Bachelor's degree	20.2	34.6	41.6
Some graduate training	4.6	9.3	3.2
Graduate or professional degree	15.7	41.8	48.0

TABLE 2.6.
Education: Survey and interview data by group (%)

	NAMC		MomsRising		MOPS		Mocha Moms		Mothers & More	
	Survey	Interviews	Survey	Interviews	Survey	Interviews	Survey	Interviews	Survey	Interviews
Less than high school (grade 11 or less)	0	0	0	0	0	0	0	0	0	0
High school diploma (including GED)	0	0	0.4	0	3.0	0	0.3	0	0.7	0
Some college, but did not graduate	6.6	8	7.8	0	11.5	0	8.5	8	4.0	8
Associate's degree (2 year degree) or specialized technical	3.3	0	5.0	4	11.4	8	5.3	4	3.6	0
Bachelor's degree	28.6	44	23.0	28	44.9	32	28.9	52	36.3	44
Some graduate training	13.2	8	10.2	0	7.7	4	11.0	0	8.6	8
Graduate or professional degree	48.4	40	53.6	68	21.4	56	45.8	36	46.7	40

TABLE 2.7.
Race: Aggregate survey and interview data (%)

	All nongroup mothers	All group mothers	
		Survey	Interviews
White (non-Hispanic)	72.8	76.1	73.6
Black (non-Hispanic)	9.7	18.2	20.8
White Hispanic	11.9	2.6	0
Black Hispanic	1.5	0.9	0.8
Asian American	2.7	2.1	1.6
Native American	1.5	0.2	0
Other	0	0	3.2

In terms of partisan identification, nongroup mothers surveyed identify mostly as Democrats (40.4%), followed by Republicans (26.5%) and Independents (22%) (tables 2.9 and 2.10). These same trends emerged for the group mothers surveyed and interviewed, except that the percentage identifying as Democratic increased to 51 percent, and Republicans dropped in number. When examining identification broken down by group, however, there are some notable differences. MOPS is overwhelmingly dominated by Republicans, with 65.1 percent of its surveyed members and 44 percent of its interviewed members expressing this political preference. None of the other groups comes close to that type of conservative-leaning identification pattern. At the opposite end of the spectrum, close to three-quarters of all MomsRising members and Mocha Moms members (both surveyed and interviewed) reported that they were Democrats. No other group leaned that heavily Democratic, although NAMC members clearly favored the Democratic Party as well.

Finally, although these data are not presented in tabular form, the overwhelming majority of mothers in this analysis were married. While approximately three-quarters of nongroup mothers surveyed reported being married, interestingly, for group mothers surveyed and interviewed, these numbers increased dramatically. Over nine out of ten group mothers reported being married, with the remaining members falling into the other relationship categories, such as civil unions, living with a partner, divorced, separated, widowed, and never married.

TABLE 2.8.
Race: Survey and interview data by group (%)

	NAMC		MomsRising		MOPS		Mocha Moms		Mothers & More	
	Survey	Interviews	Survey	Interviews	Survey	Interviews	Survey	Interviews	Survey	Interviews
White (non-Hispanic)	95	100	91.5	84	92.9	92	1.6	0	93.4	92
Black (non-Hispanic)	0.6	0	3.0	8	1.1	4	92.7	92	0.9	0
White Hispanic	1.7	0	2.6	0	3.2	0	1.0	0	3.1	0
Black Hispanic	1.7	0	0.2	0	0	0	3.9	0	0.1	4
Asian American	1.1	0	2.4	4	2.9	0	0.5	0	2.4	4
Native American	0	0	0.2	0	0	0	0.3	0	0.2	0
Other	0	0	0	4	0	4	0	4	0	0

TABLE 2.9.
Political party identification: Aggregate survey and interview data (%)

	All nongroup mothers	All group mothers	
		Survey	Interviews
Republican	26.5	25.1	12.8
Democrat	40.4	51.0	57.6
Independent	22.0	15.2	20.0
Other party	1.6	1.6	4.8
No preference	9.5	7.1	4.8

Marriage rates were highest among MOPS and Mothers & More members, with close to 100 percent of surveyed and interviewed members reporting this status, and lowest among MomsRising members, with about 80 percent of those surveyed and interviewed reporting this same status.

The mothers' organizations in this study are clearly different in many respects. Most important for the purposes of this book, although they all have an interest in the subject, they vary in how they go about promoting or advocating on behalf of workplace flexibility policies, both for their members and for society at large. They also have unique historical legacies, which shape the ways in which they view their current and future missions. These differences have produced variability in certain sociodemographic characteristics of their memberships. However, there are also significant commonalities. Across the groups, members tend to be of the same average age, with equal numbers of children. They also tend to work for pay at high levels, with the exception of MOPS members. Overall, they are also highly educated, and tend to be white, although Mocha Moms brings significant racial diversity to this population. They also tend to be overwhelmingly Democratic in their party identification (with the exception of MOPS) and settled into stable, marital relationships.

This picture of mothers' group members in the United States is thus one of a community that has many resources at its disposal in comparison with mothers not involved in these groups. This means that the group memberships have significant advantages in terms of pursuing political action to improve the quality of their lives as parents.

TABLE 2.10.
Political party identification: Survey and interview data by group (%)

	NAMC		MomsRising		MOPS		Mocha Moms		Mothers & More	
	Survey	Interviews	Survey	Interviews	Survey	Interviews	Survey	Interviews	Survey	Interviews
Republican	15.6	4	3.9	0	65.1	44	2.9	0	21.1	16
Democrat	57.2	68	72.7	72	12.9	32	71.7	72	54.8	44
Independent	19.4	20	16.3	12	12.2	16	17.2	12	15.0	36
Other party	1.1	0	3.9	16	1.5	0	0.3	16	1.5	4
No preference	6.7	8	3.3	0	8.3	8	7.9	0	7.5	0

However, while the potential for action may be clear, the members themselves might not view their participation in their groups in this same way. Therefore, it is critical to ask, how do the members currently view the role of these groups in their lives? What are the benefits they gain from participating, and what are their perspectives on their organizations' workplace flexibility goals?

3

Why Join?

It is a weekday evening in a midwestern Baptist church, where a local MOPS chapter is gathering. Ten members in total are congregating in the auditorium of the building, including a designated babysitter for the children who have been brought along.

As a way to foster the mothers' sense of accomplishment, the chapter leader had given the members very specific instructions for this meeting. All MOPS members have to exhibit whatever arts and crafts talents they have developed over time at tables set up for this purpose. Alternatively, they can participate in a talent show at the meeting. The chapter leader has also encouraged them all to "dress up" in a glamorous way for the meeting because under the stress of their parenting roles, moms rarely have the opportunity to focus on being stylish simply for their own pleasure.

Given their marching orders, two members choose to exhibit their personal creative work. One has brought handmade knitted blankets and the other samples of her photography.

The remaining members participate in the talent show, which is moderated by an emcee from MOPS. The folding chairs in the auditorium are set up for the audience and there is a stage for the performers. The chapter leader has put a bedsheet on the ground to serve as a "red carpet." All performers in the talent show have to walk down this red carpet before going onto the stage.

The acts are numerous and diverse. Several members tell jokes or do comedic sketches, others sing, and another describes how she developed talents in arts and crafts, having engaged in scrapbooking, painting, and building Christmas wreaths. The final performer leads the group in stress reduction techniques.

At the end of the show, two members dressed in clown costumes get up and start dancing to Christian rock music. They eventually begin a conga line. Within minutes, all the performers, table exhibitors, and children get in the line and start dancing around the auditorium.

When they finish dancing and go into the lobby of the church for cupcakes, several members reflect on the benefits of belonging to MOPS:

MOPS MEMBER 1: I love the group because it makes me feel less alone. It makes me feel like I am not crazy. I also get great advice about parenting because people here know what it is like to raise kids.

MOPS MEMBER 2: I love the group because it breaks up my day. It is an incredible stress reliever, too.

MOPS is a cherished part of mothers' lives across the country, as this particular snapshot of the group clearly illustrates. What benefits do members of MOPS and other mothers' organizations derive from belonging to these groups, what are their most pressing concerns, and how do the groups help alleviate the challenges presented by motherhood and paid work? Most important, what role can the organizations play in potentially influencing the public debate on workplace flexibility?

Regardless of all mothers' groups' stated missions, organizational structures, and listed activities, local chapters of these groups have significant autonomy in shaping their own character. That is, while they might be given some mandatory instructions from their national organization as well as suggestions for their curriculum, local leaders exercise considerable authority in deciding how the group will function in its own individualized meetings. Group chapters, therefore, vary from location to location in content, composition, and orientation toward their own particular goals. In this study, it is important to keep in mind that there are membership differences across the five groups as well as *within* groups, in their chapters.[1]

Because of this variability in organizational character, members may have a wide range of reasons for their own participation. Some reasons may be relatively inward-looking; that is, members engage in their organization to develop deeply cherished principles and obtain some other types of strongly held benefits that tend not to be exported outside the groups' borders. These may involve distinct types of interpersonal relationships and support, as well as other material and idea-related exchanges among members, from which nonmembers tend to be excluded.[2] The more these inward-looking resources tend to be valued by members, the more likely members are to feel as if they truly are part of a positive group dynamic.

Other members might participate in their group for relatively outward-looking goals. Like members of many of the historical mothers' organizations described in chapter 1, they want to influence business and governmental policy on important issues of the day, and they understand that their groups offer the best mechanisms for doing so. How does this outward-based orientation have meaning for its members? Or, what role can these groups play in influencing public policy?

One way to approach these questions is to examine in general how organizations operate across the American political landscape in transforming the public agenda through the relationships they have established with different policy players. The first critical relationship to explore is between these groups and two key players: members of Congress and members of the business community. Although the news media has covered the link between campaign contributions and congressional votes, what is often most important is the information transmitted from organizations to those in power.[3] While members of Congress may look first to their constituents in determining how to vote, on issues with a wider appeal, they may seek out the views of well-established interest groups.[4] In the same way, although members of the business community are primarily driven by profits, they may look to key groups for guidance on developing new ways to innovate in order to develop cutting-edge entrepreneurial practices, irrespective of their short-term costs.

The second critical relationship that groups can establish is with the general public.[5] As an issue gets placed on the policy agenda, the media will want to cover different sides of the story. Organizations can provide spokespeople for a particular side of the issue at hand. They can advocate on behalf of their ideas through various formats, such as print, television, and blogs, or through various social networking media, such as Facebook and Twitter. Once they establish their credibility as experts in a particular area, the public will react, either positively or negatively, prompting the organizations to refine their positions and sharpen their arguments even further.[6] In this iterative fashion, the public will once again have a chance to react, with organizations further adapting based on this new feedback. In this way, groups can be key actors in shaping public opinion.

The third, and most important, relationship for the discussion presented here is the relationship that the group leadership can cultivate with its members. By offering a set of clearly defined benefits for joining, the leadership can attempt to solidify loyalty and trust between themselves and their members over time.[7] These bonds become critical when the leadership needs to call on its members to engage in broader mobilization. While this might mean urging members to participate in a march, demonstration, or boycott, mobilization can take place on the much less dramatic level as well. Groups may, for example, find it more productive to provide their members with the tools they need to become effective spokespersons on behalf of their issues.[8] These tools might be talking points, leaflets, brochures, or even sample letter text that can be used when communicating with the general public, lawmakers, and the business community. In this way, members become fully engaged troops on the ground, spreading the word about the purpose and goals of the organization to which they belong.

In sum, members can achieve both inward- and outward-oriented benefits from participating in their groups. The question is, which types of benefits do they most seriously value? Do these preferences vary across NAMC, MomsRising, MOPS, Mocha Moms, and Mothers & More? And are there differences between mothers who stay at home and those who work for pay?

Why Do They Join?

Women join mothers' groups for various reasons. In the survey, all group mothers were asked, "What are the *two* most important benefits to you from being a part of your mothers' group?" As reflected in table 3.1, they were given seven possible options: emotional support, friends for me, friends for my children, information about parenting resources, information about parenting techniques, information about public policy and political activism, and other. The first five are clearly inward-oriented benefits, while the sixth—information about public policy and political activism—is an outward-oriented benefit.

In general, group mothers expressed that inward-oriented benefits were more significant to them than outward-oriented benefits. More specifically, mothers identified emotional support as the most significant benefit, followed closely by friends for them. A little over one in two mothers mentioned these as the most important features of their mothers' groups. Next, about one-quarter reported that friends for their children drew them to their mothers' group. Last, a little less than one in four mothers described information about parenting resources and techniques as important to them; about the same number rated information about public policy and political advocacy as significant in motivating them to remain part of their organizations. Interestingly, stay-at-home mothers ranked their benefits in the same way as did all group mothers in total. However, currently employed mothers reported slightly different rankings, most noticeably in their choice of information about public policy and political advocacy as compared with all mothers combined and stay-at-home mothers.

As might be expected, there were significant differences expressed among the members based on their group affiliation. Groups such as MOPS that offer substantial fellowship but only indirect advocacy in the area of workplace flexibility could be expected to attract members citing strong inward-oriented benefits but few outward-oriented benefits. Conversely, MomsRising, which provides few companionship opportunities but enormous possibilities for policy activism in advocacy for workplace flexibility could be expected to draw members citing critical outward-oriented benefits but few inward-oriented benefits. This, in fact, is the case. For example, 78.8 percent of MOPS members reported receiving emotional support as a benefit, while less than 1 percent claimed to be receiving information on public policy and political activism as a benefit. Conversely, only 19.7 percent of Moms-Rising members reported receiving emotional support from their group, but 93.4 percent asserted that they obtained public policy and political

TABLE 3.1.
Benefits from joining mothers' organizations: Results from the survey (%)

	All group mothers	All employed group mothers	All stay-at-home group mothers	NAMC	MomsRising	MOPS	Mocha Moms	Mothers & More
Emotional support	54.8	50.0	59.6	65.6	19.7	78.8	62.7	47.8
Friends for me	51.9	44.6	59.2	57.8	1.8	66.8	48.3	61.7
Friends for my children	24.0	20.1	27.9	30.0	0.2	15.0	37.6	30.3
Information about parenting resources	22.2	26.2	17.9	15.0	20.6	6.4	26.5	31.0
Information about parenting techniques	16.5	18.5	14.3	19.4	15.3	19.7	14.1	15.7
Information about public policy and political activism	16.3	22.5	9.7	4.4	93.4	0.5	4.0	5.8
Other	11.4	13.4	9.4	7.8	31.1	12.4	6.0	7.1

Note: Mothers were asked to identify the two most important benefits that they received from being a group member.

activism information as a benefit. NAMC, Mocha Moms, and Mothers & More all fell in between these extreme values in terms of the types of benefits cited by their members as important to them.

In the interviews, the mothers were asked a similar question about identifying the benefits of being part of their mothers' organizations (see table 3.2). However, here, this was an open-ended question; respondents were not given the seven options provided in the survey. As a result, the interview responses at times differed slightly from those reported in the survey. As in the survey, they named emotional support and personal friendship as their top benefits; however, in the interviews, these two themes were discussed in such a way as to be intertwined as one concept by 64 percent of the respondents. A full 19.2 percent discussed parenting information and techniques as intertwined concepts in the interviews as well. Similarly, 16 percent described information about public policy and political activism as critical to them in maintaining their membership in their groups. MOPS was once again at one extreme in terms of members citing inward-oriented but not outward-oriented benefits, while MomsRising was at the opposite end of the same spectrum. Last, in one major difference from the survey responses, instead of identifying friends for their children as a motivating force to join, 10.4 percent of mothers in the interviews described activities for their entire families as offered by their organizations as an essential benefit.

TABLE 3.2.
Reasons for joining mothers' organizations: Themes from the interviews (%)

	All group mothers	NAMC	MomsRising	MOPS	Mocha Moms	Mothers & More
Emotional support/ friends for me	64.0	76	8	96	72	64
Information about parenting resources and techniques	19.2	8	0	24	40	24
Information about public policy and political activism	16.0	0	80	0	0	0
Activities for their families	10.4	20	0	4	4	24

Note: Mothers could identify more than one benefit.

To summarize, the interview respondents identified four key benefits for them in their participating in their mothers' groups: emotional support and friends for them; information on parenting resources and techniques; information on public policy and political activism; and activities for their families. As will be demonstrated below, the members themselves spoke about these benefits in great detail when given the opportunity to reflect upon their groups' vibrant presence in their own lives.

Benefits of Group Membership:
Emotional Support and Friends for Mothers

Across the five groups and at whatever point they were in their adult life stages, members of mothers' organizations expressed a strong appreciation for the fellowship that came with group participation; this was the first most common benefit reported. By *fellowship*, some mothers meant their organizations' capacity to give them the opportunity to socialize and become energized about their responsibilities as parents. MOPS was especially useful in this regard, as it runs a special program, MOPPETS, through many of its local chapters. As described earlier, MOPPETS provides free or low-cost child care for mothers while they convene during regular organizational meeting hours. Cheryl, a thirty-year-old mother of four children, ages six and under, described how the child care offered by the MOPPETS program provided her with the peace of mind she needed to attend to her own personal needs and be revitalized as a woman, independent of her parental status.

> I just tell [the other members] how much better of a mom I feel when I leave [the meeting]. . . . It is only twice a month but I think that it's invaluable and I walk away feeling refreshed. . . . I know that my children are in a safe environment where they are being cared for and loved the way that they would be in my home. . . . I guess I feel like I am a better mom. I feel like I can do a better job of parenting. It is such a nice break. I do not feel like I am so overwhelmed. It is just energizing and refreshing.

In a similar way, Janice, thirty-seven and the mother of a seven-year-old boy and two-year-old girl, felt that the break that MOPS gave her away from her children, allowing her to be with friends, was important in invigorating her focus as a parent.

> I think part of [why I joined] was that my friends were joining, so it was a chance to be social with them and still have someone taking care of the kids. . . . The other part was the fact that . . . for one of my friends, this was something she loved and so I thought, well, I better check this out and see what this is. . . . She still, I know, always valued certain experiences that she really wanted me to have and MOPS was one of them.

Both Cheryl and Janice noted that the time spent away from their children—while knowing that they were safe—was instrumental in preventing them from becoming overwhelmed by the day-to-day tasks of motherhood. Of course, the spiritual core of MOPS' mission also gave them a God-centered direction and a sense that that the respite was necessary and productive, helping them realize the most satisfying fulfillment of their roles as mothers.

For other members, fellowship through their organization had an entirely different meaning. In many ways in American culture, motherhood is portrayed as a purely blissful state that is always 100 percent rewarding. Mothers' organizations gave women who had experiences contrary to this ideal—real-life trials that proved that parenting could be extremely frustrating—the opportunity to vent their concerns in a safe environment, free from external pressures to be perfect. Julie, forty-two years old and the mother of two girls, ages five and one, was a member of her local NAMC. She described how she could simply be herself when she was with other NAMC mothers:

> I think a Mothers' Center is one of the rare places where moms can sort of be honest about everything—you know, the good, the bad, and the ugly. . . . I'm certainly not somebody who can spend 24/7 with my child and be happy, and it's one of those few places where you could say that and not have anybody be like, "Oh, my God! Do you not love your child?" . . . I definitely do think that at its core, in society, there's sort of like a gut reaction to moms, that, you know, if they don't get this angelic look every time [their] child walks in the room, there's something wrong.

Nia, thirty-two and mother of two young girls aged six and two, described a similarly liberating experience with her group, MOPS. In Nia's perspective, mothers of her generation were not given the knowledge they need to cope with the everyday demands of parenting. Instead, in her view, women have been too focused on obtaining career success while not being properly educated about the expectations regarding the daily grind of motherhood. MOPS, to Nia, offered her a God-centered vision of how to respond to the both ups and inevitable downs of mothering.

> If you ever get the blessing of children, it is such the most wonderfully rewarding experience and yet is the sole experience that is the most exhausting, consuming job of your life. It's on both [ends of the] spectrum. You know, your child [could be] getting into a spoiled diaper in the crib and rubbing it all over and just all the crazy things toddlers do. [But] you go to MOPS and other moms are experiencing the same thing. [Then] you know you are not going crazy. . . . [Our group is designed to give] most of those mothers . . . confidence to be constructive with their children [and offer them] discipline and activities. [We want to] not just get through each day but to have a vision to [help them] guide their children into [being] productive citizens.

Just like Julie in NAMC, Nia in MOPS concluded that her organization not only gave mothers permission to be less than perfect as a parent but also the ability to feel that this imperfection was an honest way of being. The majority of mothers were not faultless, according to this perspective, and the group culture freed them to carry out their parenting tasks as the fallible human beings that they all were.

This concept of being able to let one's guard down in front of other group members meant not only being able to express feelings that were less than positive about motherhood but also being liberated from judgments about individual parenting decisions. Amy, forty-six and the mother of two boys, ages ten and thirteen, described her experiences with NAMC:

> The biggest thing for me about the Mothers' Center [is that] being a new mother, you feel so judged. . . . There is really a lot of judgment and all mothers do it. I did it, too. I did it to my sisters-in-law. [I would

say to myself about them,] "Oh, I'll never nurse when my kids have teeth, forget it. What [are they], crazy?". . . You know, things like that. And [then] you go to the Mothers' Center, [and it's different]. A very big piece of the training that moms get when they go there and attend groups [is that they] have to repeat at the beginning of every group that [they're] supposed to approach the [group] discussions in a nonjudgmental manner. [You must] keep your judgments to yourself and that creates a really safe feeling to be able to talk about [whatever you want]. . . . You know, [you can talk about] if you are breastfeeding or went natural or you had meds or whatever it is.

For Amy, this lack of judgment kept her coming back to group meetings time and again. More important, the type of open-minded attitude experienced at the meetings helped modify her own thinking about other mothers' choices about parenting. More specifically, she found that she became much more accepting about all types of mothering arrangements as a result of her participation in the group.

For other mothers, fellowship emerged as a way to compare notes on their children's developmental progress. In mothers' group meetings across the country, women learned from other mothers what each of their children was accomplishing academically, physically, and emotionally at different stages of their lives. These comparisons alerted them to any problems or difficulties they might be experiencing with their own children. One example is that of thirty-nine-year-old Paula, a member of Mothers & More who had a seven-year-old son with developmental disabilities. Going to her local mothers' organization offered her special opportunities to learn about the issues her son was facing as he proceeded throughout his daily life activities.

For me, there are not a lot of kids with any kind of development disabilities in our group. It is lovely to go and chat with other moms and hear what their completely normal, typical kids are doing. [That helps me say], "Oh, okay, so that is normal kid stuff," and to get that perspective because it is really easy to lose perspective in the world of special needs. You start to see everything as part of the problem . . . when it is [really] just kids being kids. I would say, obviously, not all the time, but in a lot of cases, kids are just kids. They do not come out as little adults but we might want them to. That has been really beneficial. The women in the group—I would hope it is this way in all groups—are very open to pretty much whatever [issues you have].

Paula thus found the group an excellent place for her to "check in" on her son's status as he grew and matured. She found her fellow members willing and able to listen, without passing judgment on her child's needs relative to those of other children.

Still other group members noted that fellowship for them simply meant that their group had a strong capacity to help facilitate solid bonds between mothers. For many women, motherhood can be an extremely isolating experience, leaving them feeling cut off from the happenings of the public world. Judy, a thirty-seven-year-old mother of two preschool children and a MOPS member, had a particularly difficult time as a military wife. She constantly was relocating with her spouse—every two to three years—and found it difficult to make new friends. Luckily, she found that during her last move, MOPS had provided her with the friendships that she so desperately wanted.

> I have made some really good friends through MOPS here and actually, my MOPS friends are probably my closest friends here. [Being a military mom poses its own challenges. Before MOPS,] sometimes finding a friend [made me think], is it really worth it to get very close, because you are going to be hurt when you leave [her]? . . . [Also], sometimes things do not come together until your very last year. You can be in some place for three or four years and it is not until your last year that you are actually really comfortable in that location and you really start to think of it as home. [But] then you have to . . . leave again. Being at MOPS [was different.] Within the first six months that I had moved out here . . . and had joined MOPS, I have found some really great friends that I know I will keep in touch with when I leave.

Shirley, forty-two and the mother of two young boys, ages eight and four, echoed this theme when she described her feelings about Mocha Moms:

The number one benefit I get from being a part of Mocha Moms is the relationships I get to form with other moms. . . . I have relationships from when I joined eight years ago . . . but each year new moms come in and they have children who are the age of my children. They may have just had a new child, and now this is their first time joining, because when they had their first child, Mocha Moms wasn't around or they didn't find it at that time. And so we [constantly] meet new moms.

These friendships were especially meaningful because they were based on the shared role of motherhood, which immediately fostered a common experience of challenges that some members believed only other mothers could comprehend. Michelle, a thirty-one-year-old Mocha Moms mother of a two-year-old son, made the following observation on this point:

[Mocha Moms helps with spreading an] understanding of a lifestyle of a mom that is just different from a woman who is not a mom. Yes—and we're talking about daily experiences. You know, [these experiences include] why you can't go out for cocktails on Wednesday at nine o'clock. [They include] when you're excited when your child takes a first step and your non-mom friends really couldn't care less. They don't get it. Or when [your children are] fully potty trained and you no longer have to go out and buy Pampers. And also the support [that you receive], you know, when they're teething or if there is something else going on that you don't really know what to do, you ask them, and there's at least one mom who can come back with an on-target response.

For mothers like Michelle, then, group membership provided fellowship in the form of strong friendships with other mothers. This did not mean that Michelle was not open to relationships with non-mothers; however, she reported that she often tired of explaining the routine of her life to those whom she believed would be unable to relate to it. Fortunately for her, her organization gave her an automatic platform of understanding among women whose lives had many commonalities.

Benefits of Group Membership: Information about Parenting Resources and Techniques

The second most common benefit of group participation reported by mothers in the interviews involved information they received that they felt was central in their becoming the best parents they could be. Whether they were first-time mothers or experienced mothers facing unexpected challenges, these women sought out fellow group members to guide them in taking the best possible care of their children.

Some groups provided formal mechanisms for educating mothers about issues likely to be critical to them as their children passed through assorted developmental stages. For example, Amber, a thirty-one-year-old mother of four children aged six and under, described how MOPS organized a series of speakers to educate mothers on topics of interest for its members. Most notably for Amber, these speakers simply assumed that all mothers wanted to do their best in raising their children.

> The number one benefit [of being a MOPS member] is that I've met some really neat people and then I think I've learned some good things [from the MOPS speakers]. . . . Let me try to pull a few out [of my memory] that I can [describe], or the ones that stuck with me. One was just talking about developmental issues with kids. [This speaker was] talking about . . . appropriate ways to engage your kids. [The speaker also relayed how] different kids like to play with different things and just things you can do around the house with them. You know, like one kid may like to play with a pile of Tupperware and that's okay. . .You know? . . . And [your first] kid may sit and play with the same toys for hours and your next child may not sit and play with anything for longer than two minutes [and both are okay].

As reflected in Amber's and other interviews, such formal events helped mothers gain more confidence in parenting children with different strengths, abilities, and interests. The message frequently communicated from these forums was that each child was unique and mothers should understand that each child possessed an individualized maturation path that was completely "normal" for that child.

Other mothers cited the importance of less formal mechanisms of relaying advice, such as the simple peer-to-peer education that they found in their own personal groups. This was critical because even women who have been mothers for a long time can encounter new problems with raising their children and want to seek out others who are ready, willing, and able to help. In this way, mothers' organizations are an excellent resource in providing a pool of knowledge created by fellow mothers that can be tapped during uncertain times. Margaret, forty-one and the mother of a seven-year-old girl, was a member of Mocha Moms. She articulated her satisfaction with using other group members to help her answer her child-rearing questions:

> Currently I would say the benefit [of participating] is, I still have the issue of coming across something with my child for the very first time. Yes, I've been a mom for seven years but things will still pop up that I have never dealt with before and I like to be able to [handle them]. . . . Even if I can't make it to the support groups during the day because I'm at work, I can send an e-mail out [saying], "Have you guys ever had this before?" Or, "Is your child wearing deodorant yet?" Or, "Is this common or [not]?" . . . "Is this supposed to happen?". . . "What is the age when kids stop asking this?" "Why are we supposed to do that?" I need to be able to send an e-mail out [and I can with Mocha Moms]. . . . Of course, you always get a response back because we're very active online as well as in person. . . . We just need to talk. . . . [I can ask] other moms who have older kids [questions as well]. I could ask a question about . . . what age did your child start playing on the Internet or when did you let your child have a cell phone? You know, [my kids might ask], "Mom, can I have a cell phone?" [And I can confidently answer,] "Well, no, you're seven."

As Margaret's experiences suggest, the groups' ability to provide information does not end at each local chapter's door. Online capabilities enable some members to post their concerns to the entire national network of chapters in the organization. A member of Mothers & More, Diana, thirty-four, had two daughters, one two years old and the other eighteen months, and she was expecting a new baby shortly. Diana explained that she first used the group as a source of advice when she was trying to introduce her daughters to the concept of sharing a bedroom. However, the most recent pressing source of anxiety in her life was that her father, before he passed away, had Parkinson's disease and needed her attention. She recalled how she had difficulty balancing the needs of her father and of her children at this point in her life and she turned toward the group for support:

> One of the cool things [that] I did not realize when I joined is that there are message boards in the main website and [one is dedicated to] toddlers and mothers with elderly parents. . . . [Even though my parents were not elderly, I used the site]. . . . It was [difficult] juggling one, then two kids, and a father with Parkinson's, who was deteriorating. [To cope, I] just totally sounded off on a message board. It was so strange. The day my dad died, I said to myself, "I need to call Charlotte." There was this woman Charlotte and I never met her before. I had [only] talked to her on these boards. She is older than I am but she just knew my situation. She has the same situation and out of that we became friends. My best friend and I have been friends since I was five but [Charlotte] was the one [I wanted to call]. I was like, "I have to call Charlotte." I always think about that. What a strange turn of events.

Diana thus depended on Charlotte at a crisis point without ever having met her. The shared information between the two—and the commonality of a similar struggle of caregiving—had transcended the need to be connected in person. This, in Diana's mind, demonstrated the true power of her mothers' group.

For other mothers, the group went beyond providing direct answers to parenting questions that were relatively straightforward. It went further by offering mothers opportunities to share *different parenting approaches to common problems* that might be more useful in tackling a current difficulty. A member of Mothers & More, Rachel, thirty-five years old and with a three-year-old son and a baby on the way, found her local chapter to be an incredibly rich source of information on multiple ways to handle issues that often come up with newborn children.

> Along with the camaraderie and the friendship [at Mothers & More], just the advice is enormous. When you are having problems with your kids, [for example, if] they are not sleeping well at night, [group members] offer different perspectives. Everybody has a different parenting style. Just exposing ourselves to that [is helpful], to maybe think, "Well, maybe the approach that I am taking in parenting my child is

not necessarily working, but this other person is able to offer a different approach."

Rachel's remarks illustrate how the exchange of different philosophies about parenting techniques could help many group members in raising their children; the group setting also created an environment whereby ideas were met with receptivity and acceptance, a theme that was repeated throughout the interviews here.

Benefits of Group Membership: Information about Public Policy and Political Activism

The third most common benefit for some women in participating in mothers' organizations was information about public policy and activism. Not surprisingly, this theme emerged in the interviews solely among members of MomsRising, an organization primarily dedicated to raising awareness on issues such as workplace flexibility. The organization was central in the lives of a number of mothers because of its usefulness in addressing critical concerns affecting parents across the board. According to Connie, a thirty-three-year-old mother of a three-year-old boy, MomsRising kept her apprised of matters that she was likely to care about as a mother.

> I think I feel like I am really informed about certain pieces of legislation or just certain issues. I feel like the [group] gives attention and brings to my attention things that I may not otherwise have on my radar. I like to be pretty involved. I consider myself pretty well read and informed, but the [group] shines a light on things that are important to families and present causes for action that otherwise I may not be partaking in.

For mothers like Connie, the information MomsRising offers to them would never come from the mainstream media, and this extra analysis offered by the group is critical in building their political muscle. The fact that MomsRising is an online group dedicated to advocacy on behalf of mothers' issues—rather than being a more generalized parents' rights group—made it especially attractive to members who wished to see concrete proposals come to fruition in the form of family-friendly laws and policies. Carmen, a thirty-year-old member of MomsRising with a six-year-old daughter, explained her attraction to the group.

> I get news [from MomsRising] that is directly relevant to me as . . . a mother. I also [gain] awareness because I rely on the news [that MomsRising provides] sometimes. That is when I realize, oh, wait a minute . . . why do I not know about this from the mainstream media? This is also the time that I fill in the gaps that are not reported, that are not discussed, or are not raised [by the mainstream media].

While Connie and Carmen both looked to their group to provide much needed information about political concerns, it is also critical to note that group members did not necessarily agree with the positions taken by the organization on every issue under its umbrella. However, there were enough key issues that struck a positive chord with most members and encouraged them to remain involved.

Furthermore, many mothers described the most important role of the group as providing them with much needed, easily accessible information in a world in which they were crunched for time. Mothers with small children in particular reported being overwhelmed with tasks to accomplish every day simply in order to provide and care for their families. For this set of mothers, MomsRising was a vehicle to facilitate the exchange of policy information for mothers who are constantly on the go. Angel, a forty-year-old mother of a fourteen-year-old daughter and another daughter aged seven, described the ease of knowledge transmission:

> Really and truly, [MomsRising] puts issues . . . like right in my face because [the information] comes right into my e-mail box. I don't have to go searching for this because I don't have time. I do not have time. I barely have time to go to the grocery store. [MomsRising] puts the issue right there so if I want to look at it, right then, first thing in the morning, I can. If I think, oh, gosh, that is kind of interesting, but I really do not have time to follow through on that, then it's at least in the back of my mind which is more than I can say for [what the mainstream news provides]. . . . I don't watch [the news] because it

is too depressing. [MomsRising] puts the issues that as a woman, as a mother, as a working mom but who understands about stay-at-home moms—it just puts it all right there for me. When you watch the [mainstream] news, sometimes you are like, man, that is so biased, so not right, and the stuff that I get from MomsRising, I can really see what the issue is. Does that make sense?

Like other mothers in the study, Angel looked to her group to provide her with information that she was unlikely to find on her own. The e-mail alerts, blogs, and regularly updated website of MomsRising made her task of keeping up on issues such as workplace flexibility much easier.

Finally, some women found that once they became mothers, their eyes were really opened to the ways in which public policies seemed to be stacked against them in their caregiving roles. In other words, their experience of motherhood became a period of political awakening and MomsRising gave them the means by which to turn their sights on law-makers and other decision makers who had the power to change their lives in a positive way. For many years, Diamond, forty-six years old and the mother of a six-year-old daughter, had been a lawyer in a high-powered firm. However, she, like other female attorneys with whom she worked, constantly felt under pressure to hide her family respon-sibilities for fear of not being taken seriously by her male bosses. She eventually left the firm and began working in the nonprofit advocacy world so that she could have more flexibility. As she reported, she even had her personal story featured on the MomsRising website.

My participation is more in reading the e-mails and sending letters to my legislators, forwarding stuff to people. . . . It's a good way for me to be alerted about issues that are relevant to me and it makes me feel really good. . . . Until I became a parent, I just didn't really know how stacked the system was against [mothers]. . . . I went to very high-ranked schools and was always educationally successful. . . . [I] never had a real gender discrimination experience before and it was not until I was home on maternity leave that all of a sudden I just . . . felt like men have been playing this scam on women for all these years. So I think to me having a political movement that harnesses that kind of frustration is an effective tool.

In a similar way, Sheila, thirty-one and the mother of a seven-year-old girl and a seven-month-old boy, described the group's power in organizing large numbers of women to press for political change in the areas affecting mothers who work for pay.

> Yes, I think [MomsRising] made me more aware of other women's plights—like I am not alone. I am not the only one who thinks day care should be more affordable and more accessible and I am not the only one who is having a rough time with finances. I am not the only single mom out there who has good sense and is not like a single, teenaged, uneducated person.

Both Diamond and Sheila both hoped that by pulling together their efforts, like other mothers in MomsRising, they would ultimately achieve a sense of accomplishment in the form of different public policy reforms, including workplace flexibility.

Benefits of Group Membership: Family-centric Activities

The fourth most common theme that emerged from the interviews regarding benefits involved the groups' providing recreational activities for members' families. This theme overlapped somewhat with one identified in the survey, where respondents identified "friends for their children" as a key benefit of group membership. However, in the interviews, respondents discussed activities both for them as mothers by themselves and activities focused on their families as entire units.

For some members, the mother-only activities became essential after a period when they felt that they were devoting a lot of their efforts toward mothering and were neglecting personal care. Kathleen, forty-nine years old and the mother of a ten-year-old daughter, was a member of NAMC. Like most other parents, she found the tasks of motherhood daunting at times, and she looked to her local chapter to provide her with more adult-oriented diversions.

> I am pretty involved in the financial committee [of our group] so I've gotten to know some of the younger mothers through that, which

has been nice. . . . The main group that I'm in is a book group, and it's just, you know, something I really look forward to. We meet once a month. . . . We've read a lot of great books and things that I never would have read without the suggestions of other people.

Similarly, Emily, thirty-five and the mother of two boys, ages three and five, found that Mothers & More helped her by giving her mother-centric activities to do. For her, the emotional connection offered to her by mothers who were going through the same experiences of parenthood made these activities even more meaningful.

I would say for me, my husband is great, but to have other women who have actually gone through being a mom and just have transitioned with their careers too, [is especially important to me] [I enjoy] just the social support of other people. . . . That has been really great. Mothers & More is really big on having the moms do stuff without the kids . . . which is really nice. We have a lot of moms' nights out and couples' nights out and stuff like that. Of course, [most of the activities] revolve around the kids and we have family events as well. [But it is also about] taking care of yourself so that you can be a better parent.

Kathleen and Emily articulated specific benefits of group participation that were common across a sizeable number of the respondents: the need for adult-oriented activities in a world where they found themselves focusing very heavily on child-oriented activities. Meeting up with other mothers without child care responsibilities distracting them was therefore essential to their general well-being as they tried to lead well-rounded lives.

Finally, some mothers discussed the role of their organizations as central in finding new things to do with their children. What was key for these mothers was that these innovative activities need not cost large sums of money. Organizations such as Mothers & More directed members to inexpensive options that otherwise might not have been on their radar screens in terms of outlets for their children. Selena, thirty-eight and the mother of three children under the age of seven, described this benefit:

[It's all about doing something] that I may not have otherwise forced myself to do unless it were organized. . . . I learned about some new parks in town and I used to take my kids [there as a result of the group]. [At Mothers & More] I just [have] the chance to connect with other like-minded women and moms in our local community.

Groups such as Mothers & More gave women the opportunity to learn about options to have fun with their children but with a unique twist— the group stressed low-cost entertainment possibilities that did not require significant effort. This was important because many mothers reported feeling somewhat stuck by inertia after having their children; they were getting caught up in the daily tasks of child rearing and were unable to move beyond their "typical" activities. By organizing events or presenting information about outings, the groups moved these mothers in a positive direction toward trying something new, hopefully to the benefit of all involved.

Many American mothers today have the chance to participate in various organizations that tend to attract women based on their current level of paid labor force participation. No group is "pure"; each has as members mothers who work for pay and mothers who stay at home. Not surprisingly, those groups with higher percentages of mothers working for pay have more aggressive public policy goals of reforming workplaces, making them more flexible environments, among other mother-friendly goals. Yet is this why mothers are joining? To change the world?

When asked about the benefits that they received from their organizations, the largest number of respondents from all groups in both the survey and interviews identified emotional support/friends for them, followed by information related to parenting resources and techniques. Only then did members discuss information related to public policy and political activism as they pertain to issues such as workplace flexibility. Finally, friends for their children and a derivative theme, family-centric activities, had somewhat different ranks in the survey and interviews.

Overall, then, while inward-oriented benefits are clearly important, it is puzzling why outward-oriented benefits are not identified more prominently by these members (with the exception of MomsRising members), especially given each group's relatively clear-cut position on the topic of workplace flexibility. One explanation might be that each group is somewhat reluctant to proactively engage its membership in the workplace flexibility arena, for fear that it may divide its own set of stay-at-home members and members who work for pay. That is, perhaps each organization's leadership is worried about pitting mother against mother within its own ranks. Is this a realistic fear? Do members of mothers' groups hold such strong opinions of others' work and life arrangements that workplace flexibility reform, even in the form advocated by their own organizations, is a nonstarter?

4

Do Mommy War Attitudes Prevent Organizing?

On a cool evening in September, twelve members of Mothers & More come together at a local independent living residence for senior citizens that also has an assisted living component. The meeting is taking place in a small dining area, with lots of snacks on the table. As the members enjoy their food, the older residents walk by and sometimes stick their heads in the room to find out exactly what is happening. After ten minutes, the guest speaker—an expert in the field of childhood development—introduces herself, with members listening attentively. She begins to explore a potentially volatile topic: being nervous about one's own parenting techniques and, perhaps at the same time, being judgmental of others' methods. Of course, these issues can be even more hotly debated when the subject of a mother's paid working status is added to the mix.

GUEST SPEAKER: I am a specialist in family studies. I am also a mother, wife, and grandmother. I used to be a professor of family studies and now I am a life coach as well. Being a parent is the hardest and most important job on the planet. I am here tonight as a resource. There is not a right or wrong way to parent. But there are effective and ineffective ways to parent. There are also legal and illegal ways to parent. I want to give you permission to be human. There is too much stress over parenting. I want you to let up on yourself and let up on your kids where possible. Take a deep breath. Let's go around and say who you are.

Mothers & More Member 1: I have a four-year-old boy. He is not an easy kid.

Mothers & More Member 2: I have three kids. They are eleven, nine, and four. They are at different stages and I need help.

Mothers & More Member 3: I have a three-year-old girl and twin boys who are two. I want to get out of the house. I want to get through this difficult time and also deal with their sibling rivalry.

Mothers & More Member 4: I have three kids, ages five, three, and one. They are good kids. But I have found that after I had the baby, I am snapping at the older girls. I have tried to be more positive. My husband is not around much [and I am a stay-at-home mom]. I have been trying to be happier. This group helps me feel not alone. I did do something bad lately—I screamed at my kids. But part of me felt good that I screamed at them . . .

Mothers & More Member 5: [As a working mom], I have a three-year-old boy and I want information on how to handle him. . . . My kid bit someone today in day care.

What does it mean to be the perfect mother in American society today? Is there such a thing as a perfect mother? Did these Mothers & More members seem to have the answers? Why is it that most mothers want to achieve this goal of parenting without errors? How do they believe they should best organize their lives to maximize their potential as mothers? What is the role of paid work in being the "perfect" mother? Does it help mothers achieve their goals or thwart them? Do mothers hold such strong views on this topic that organizations may be unwilling to enter this debate and promote the goal of workplace flexibility to the best of their ability for fear of alienating some of their members?

As the dialogue from the Mothers & More meeting suggests, American mothers today are harried. They always seem to be on the go, bringing their children from activity to activity, making sure that they are excelling in school, and directing them toward higher levels of achievement in all their pursuits. This was not always the case in American history. In the nineteenth century, the United States was a much more rural country, with a farm-based economy. Parents viewed children as mini-adults, capable of sharing most of the emotional and physical demands experienced by grownups. They were expected to work hard on the farm and contribute productively to the household.[1]

By the end of the nineteenth century and beginning of the twentieth, the effects of industrialization had pushed many families to leave their farms and move into urban areas. During this period, mothers began to view their children in different ways from those of the past. No longer were children to be valued primarily for their economic contribution to the family unit. Instead, mothers saw their children for the first time as beings with their own unique sets of needs and concerns. These included reaching developmental milestones at a set pace, acquiring social skills, and generally becoming good citizens. Reflecting the changing attitudes of the times, lawmakers worked to pass laws dictating compulsory school attendance and regulations against child labor. Entire communities would now be geared toward making sure that all children's talents were nurtured and never exploited.

The primary burden of investing in children in this way was placed at the feet of mothers. They began to engage in "intensive mothering," which involved devoting all their time and energy to the enrichment of their children.[2] These practices became especially evident in middle-class families, where children's lives began to be run entirely by the calendar.[3] In contrast to mothers in working-class families, where "free play" was encouraged, middle-class mothers began to fill their children's schedules with sports practices, games, playdates, and tutoring appointments. To achieve the goal of maximum engagement, mothers had to spend an extraordinary amount of time planning out the hours of each day, from dropping off and picking up their children to overseeing each of their activities. But mothers' work became more labor intensive in another way as well. Middle-class mothers became committed to teaching their children to capitalize on the rewards of this world by learning how to effectively communicate with adults. In doing so, mothers had to spend an extraordinary amount of time verbally engaging with their children so they could learn the rules of the negotiating game in life. The ultimate hope was to provide their children with every possible advantage in schooling, social situations, and the world of work.

Intensive mothering thus became the norm of middle-class parenting in the United States and all mothers were expected to heed its dictates or be judged negatively. However, it was not the only factor through which society came to judge mothers. The women's movement of the 1960s and 1970s encouraged women to pursue their own dreams by obtaining a fulfilling occupation. The average woman would thus have "market worth," just like her male counterparts. However, as described in chapter 1, the jobs available in the American labor market are often open to only ideal workers. Ideal workers are able to devote themselves twenty-four hours a day, seven days a week, to their job.[4] These workers must be on call to their employers and have no serious competing obligations on their time. Work, in essence, must become their life, so that the goals of the corporate world can be achieved most effectively.

How do mothers, then, meet two very different standards of performance in today's society? Do they focus on intensive mothering only, and risk being seen as failing miserably in their paid work and being constantly devalued?[5] Or do they concentrate on their paid work, and risk being seen as failing miserably in the intensive mothering part of their lives? Or do they attempt to juggle both roles, while being constantly afraid of not measuring up in either?[6]

Clearly, the choices for mothers are not easy, and, as noted earlier, these conflicts have generated what many in the media have called the Mommy Wars.[7] The Mommy Wars pit stay-at-home mothers who have foregone their careers, at least temporarily, against mothers who work for pay either by choice or through necessity.[8] While some have argued that these "wars" are created solely by journalists and talking heads, a small number of qualitative studies have shown that certain mothers truly do internalize mother-related employment-based distinctions and expectations.[9] More educated mothers with challenging careers in front of them also experience these pressures.[10] To survive day to day in a seemingly unwinnable situation, they each define the ideal mother from the standpoint of the role they themselves play. That is, stay-at-home mothers emphasize that good mothers should be completely self-sacrificing to their children's needs, while employed mothers stress that mothers who are happy and fulfilled in their work pursuits make the best parents.

However, not all mothers embrace one particular view of the ideal mother, as other research has demonstrated. Factors that might heighten feelings of disapproval toward mothers with different arrangements are varied and complex. For instance, mothers may be less opposed to others' arrangements if they are more satisfied with their own lives, are less guilty, and do not feel as if they have made major personal sacrifices to be where they are.[11] Another factor is interpersonal support: if mothers feel that they have strong familial ties and solid friendships that help them lead their lives in the way they see fit, they might be less likely to judge others.[12] Women whose own mothers worked for pay also might be less likely to judge others, while African American women and women with lesser means who have historically either desired to work or had to work in greater numbers might demonstrate fewer judgments as well.[13] By contrast, exposure to media that offers only one-dimensional views of mothers' opposing arrangements can heighten Mommy War sentiments.[14]

This chapter addresses understanding the breadth and depth of these Mommy Wars feelings among mothers' groups members, as well as the exact nature of the judgments that have developed over time. Most important for this chapter is assessing if Mommy War attitudes may be preventing mothers' groups from promoting a more visible and potent workplace flexibility agenda, or if it is a much overblown problem that group leaders should immediately cast aside and choose to move forward with their workplace flexibility goals.

The Depth and Intricacies of the Mommy Wars

To assess the depth of Mommy War sentiments among women who have joined mothers' groups in the United States, the survey probed members about what they viewed as the most "ideal arrangement" between work and family life. The survey defined an ideal arrangement as one that works best for most people. The specific question was "Do you believe that there is one ideal arrangement in terms of whether mothers should stay at home to care for their children or work outside the home for pay?"

Table 4.1 demonstrates that a significant majority of mothers' group members do *not* believe that that there is only one ideal arrangement for all families in terms of combining child rearing and paid work. This is a new and compelling finding that has not been documented

TABLE 4.1.
Is there one ideal arrangement for children? Aggregate and group survey data (%)

	All group mothers	All employed group mothers	All stay-at-home group mothers	NAMC	MomsRising	MOPS	Mocha Moms	Mothers & More
Yes	18.5	15.7	21.5	17.6	10.6	28.3	24.8	12.8
No	81.5	84.3	78.5	82.4	89.4	71.7	75.2	87.2

in previous studies. For all group members considered together, 81.5 percent disagreed with the notion that there is only one ideal arrangement, with only 18.5 percent agreeing. Notably, mothers who are currently employed and mothers who stay at home had remarkably similar attitudes. In addition, high levels of disagreement with this "ideal arrangement" statement occurred within each group, ranging from 71.7 percent of MOPS members to 89.4 percent of MomsRising members.

For those members who *did* believe that there was one ideal arrangement for mothers, among all group members, they expressed the most support for mothers working part time (39.1%), followed by mothers staying at home (33.5%) (see table 4.2). About one-quarter of respondents expressed a preference for another type of arrangement, and only 2.1 percent selected mothers working full time. Overall, employed mothers saw as ideal mothers working part time, while stay-at-home mothers mostly favored the at-home option. Finally, in each organization, the largest percentage of mothers asserted a preference for the part-time option, with the exception of MOPS members, who valued mothers staying at home the most.

To uncover some of these nuances in these attitudes, in the interviews mothers were asked if they ever felt it was hard to talk to their friends who are mothers and who have made different choices from theirs regarding the balance of paid work and parenting in their lives. They were also asked if they felt judged about their own decisions, or even if they themselves engaged in judging behavior. In response, mothers reported different types of judgment for different reasons. But expressing the most common set of beliefs, just as in the survey, a plurality of all group mothers stated that they possessed no Mommy War attitudes at all—another critical, important new finding (see table 4.3). Indeed, only a plurality of Mothers & More members expressed a higher percentage of judgments versus nonjudgments.

No Mommy War Attitudes: Trying to Get Along

For the most significant number of mothers in the interviews, Mommy War attitudes were not a problem as they perceived and constructed their daily lives. How did they remove this issue as a point of contention among family and friends? Some mothers simply agreed to

TABLE 4.2.
What do you think that one ideal arrangement is? Aggregate and group survey data (%)

	All group mothers	All employed group mothers	All stay-at-home group mothers	NAMC	MomsRising	MOPS	Mocha Moms	Mothers & More
Mothers working full time	2.1	4.2	0.57	0	4.2	0.93	3.2	2.4
Mothers working part time	39.1	46.2	33.5	56.3	41.7	29.9	39.6	47.6
Mothers not working at all outside the home	33.5	21.5	42.4	18.8	25.0	54.2	18.2	25.9
Other	25.4	27.9	23.5	25.0	29.2	15.9	39.0	24.1

TABLE 4.3.
Types of Mommy War judgments: Themes from the interviews (%)

	All group mothers	NAMC	MomsRising	MOPS	Mocha Moms	Mothers & More
No Mommy War judgments: trying to get along	33.6	28	24	28	60	28
Antiworking judgment: mothers should be at home with their children	16.8	4	24	12	12	32
Antiworking judgment: mothers as alienated in their communities	13.6	20	20	12	12	4
Anti-stay-at-home judgment: mothers as not contributing to society	14.4	12	8	24	4	24
Anti-stay-at-home judgment: mothers as "relaxing" all day	11.2	8	24	8	8	8

disagree. Crystal was a fifty-two-year-old member of Mothers & More and a stay-at-home mother of two daughters, ages ten and five. She had a very strong belief that mothers should be at home with their children. However, she prided herself on behaving with "tolerance" toward others who decided to work for pay.

> No, I do not have a problem [with Mommy War attitudes]. If [other mothers] have chosen to [work], that is their choice and they usually know that I would not choose that. I am perfectly open with my opinion. That is what tolerance is. . . . I do not agree with them and they know [that] I do not agree with them. I think my way is right. They believe their way is right. Tolerating does not mean that you agree; it means that you are tolerating an opposite point of view. That is okay. I have friends who are opposite from me in many different ways. Sometimes I explain to them what tolerance is and they are like, "Oh, yes." I do not have to agree with you but I am not going to not be your friend if I have chosen to do something else.

Like Crystal, other mothers had strong opinions but, instead of being vocal about their differences, decided that it was best to keep the topic out of conversations completely. Christina, a MOPS member aged thirty-seven and a stay-at-home mother of three young boys under the age eight, described her strategy.

> I avoid that topic [of working versus staying at home] because I guess I see that as an area where, clearly, we [may] disagree. But, you know, if somebody really wants to talk about the pros and cons of the issue, then I would gladly enter that conversation. But in casual conversation, or just you know . . . with friends, I'm not going to bring up something that divides us. . . . So, I would say [that] I just avoid the topic.

For Crystal and Christina, and for other mothers in the study, differences of opinion on whether mothers should work for pay or stay at home were strong. However, they each employed their own effective strategies to handle the potentially conflictual issue in their interactions with friends.

While Crystal and Christina understood these differences as particularly divisive and used their own strategies to avoid confrontation, other mothers discovered that Mommy War attitudes were not a problem because they had learned to live in each other's shoes. Deborah, a Mocha Moms member and thirty-three years old, had a five-year-old son and a three-year-old daughter. At the time of her interview, she worked part time as a fund-raiser for a nonprofit organization. She cherished the fact that Mommy War attitudes did not affect her life, and she attributed this to the nature of the friendships she had developed over time. These friendships exposed her to different potential ways of organizing her life and made her realize that there were a variety of ways mothers could excel at parenting.

> [I don't experience Mommy War attitudes in my life], but I would definitely say that just comes from very high-quality friendships. I'm sort of lucky in that way, I think. A lot of my friends [have] had different experiences with work and work-life balance, and we're able to all support each other. And everyone's sort of in a different circumstance. I think I am probably the only one who works part time. The other three work full time. Then one, at one point, was a stay-at-home mom. So it's been different. You know, I think we've all been able to support each other through our different experiences. . . . And I've never been judged, thank goodness, by my friends, anyway.

Ellen, a MomsRising member with two daughters, ages four and two, also worked for pay, had the same experience with her friends. Indeed, she found that she and her friends constantly educated each other about the challenges and rewards of each situation, staying at home or working for pay.

> Recently a friend of mine, who is a stay-at-home mom, said, "It really made me rethink what it would be like to be a working mom because I always [used to] think of [working moms as] these moms who send their kids off to some nanny and then disappear for nine hours. But you figured out a way of not doing that, and it's made me rethink that whole thing." I think that for the most part, like 99 percent of the time in any situation, moms understand that other moms

are doing the best they can and they're struggling. It's wonderful but it's certainly not easy. We just need to be supportive of each other in whatever is going on.

As a thirty-nine-year-old mother of two young children, Ellen had a lot on her plate, but she found strength in friendships with women from different backgrounds who were truly willing to listen to and learn from other mothers' experiences.

Anti–Working-Mother Judgment: Mothers Should Be at Home with their Children

Not all mothers' group members were lucky enough to be protected against criticism for their work-family arrangements, but, as stated earlier, the number of women expressing judgmental attitudes was much smaller than those without such attitudes. When these attitudes did emerge, mothers working for pay were the focal point of several negative judgments as they combined employment with raising their children. The first and most common theme emerging from the interviews in this category was the feeling that these mothers should not be working at all. The second was that these mothers were subjected to alienation in their own communities through their "choice" of working, discussed below.

No matter where in the country they lived or what type of job they had, mothers who worked for pay reported facing enormous pressure to be at home with their children. Jada, thirty-one years old and with a two-year-old son, thoroughly enjoyed her job as a customer service representative, working twenty hours a week. Through specific arrangements with her company, she was able to route directly to her home the calls she received, enabling her to work and care for her son at the same time. She felt judged, however, for not being absolutely focused on her son all the time.

> I think that everybody has to make her own choices. If somebody . . . tries to tell me my choices are wrong . . . I can walk away from it. But I definitely know people [who disagree with me]. With moms' groups, you know, there's the grapevine. You know, I've heard different

rumblings about people being appalled that I don't thoroughly enjoy staying home with my son and that I don't take away from it what I should. And that's their opinion and that's fine, but they've never addressed it with me. . . . [But] I know that there are people who do have problems [with my working].

Interestingly, for Jada judgment came from the "grapevine," through her membership with a mothers' group, rather than from friends and acquaintances outside her group. This theme of Mommy War attitudes coming from the organizations themselves emerged in several interviews, but it definitely was not an overriding one. More often than not, judgment came from sources outside the group context.

Other mothers felt that they were being judged for working not because they did not "enjoy" their children, but because their lives did not "revolve" around their children. Rosa, thirty-nine, was a member of MomsRising and had a two-year-old daughter. She took great pride in her job as a college professor, which of course had required a prior investment of years of education. While she viewed her life as multifaceted and quite positive, she often felt that others viewed her less favorably for having career interests of her own.

I'm in a playgroup on Tuesday afternoon with other kids who are my daughter's age, and many of [the mothers] are stay-at-home moms. I feel that I don't have so much to talk to them [about] sometimes. They are nice people but they are not going to become my closest friends. Most of them used to work for pay until they had a child. . . . I would say that most of the parents are stay-at-home parents in my neighborhood. I don't think that they think that working moms are evil. I don't think that they are like, "Oh, you go to work, [so] your kid is being neglected." There are a lot of moms who work part time here and who send their kid to day care one or two days a week, or use the nanny a little, and they are trying to keep their hand in something even though they are not really staying home. . . . I just think one of the things that I talk about is work so people who are staying at home, their life revolves around their child. As much as I love my child, that is not my whole life so that makes it a little more difficult to really bond with people who are home all of the time.

For Rosa, the signals that she received from other mothers in her community were complex. She knew that she somehow was being cast as "different" from the other mothers in the neighborhood, but she did not sense that these judgments were completely negative. Instead, she speculated that part of what motivated these other mothers in treating her differently was a sense of envy over her career. In her view, these were women who believed that mothers should stay at home but at the same time missed the intellectual challenge of their former jobs.

Another way the theme of mothers being expected to remain at home emerged was through the issue of day care. This was often a hot-button issue among mothers involved in this study, with many mothers expressing strong views, either in favor of or opposed to using such services. Mothers who worked for pay found themselves particularly targeted when they elected to use day care. Rita was a thirty-one-year-old member of MomsRising and the mother of a four-year-old girl and a one-year-old boy. She was earning her PhD in political science and teaching as an adjunct professor at a local university to earn some extra money. She described her experience with the day care issue:

> I was at a birthday party with my daughter, and I was talking to a mom who has four kids. I was like, "Oh my God, I can't even just balance two! It's crazy!" We were talking about some things and one of her younger sons just started in the same nursery school as my daughter. She was asking me if I was going to send my son and I said that I was going to wait and see. He is in day care right now and I will just see if he will be ready. [Maybe he will be ready], maybe not. Well, she was so quick to say, "None of my children ever went to day care." I was somewhat like, What is that supposed to mean? What am I supposed to do with him? I did not respond because sometimes I feel like those conversations are not productive. I think that sometimes people feel inferior [because of their choices]. I was not trying to make her feel inferior but I think that is what it is. It comes from that.

Notable about Rita's experience is that she felt that she had a foot in the door of the working world and a foot in the door of the stay-at-home world, because of the flexible nature of her job. In conversations such as the one she related above, she described herself as being tested on where her feet were more fully planted. In this case, whether or not she pursued this particular method of taking care of her children then became the litmus test for whether she was perceived as a good mother.

Anti–Working-Mother Judgment: Mothers as Alienated in Their Communities

As noted above, the second most common judgment lodged against mothers who worked for pay was that through their employment arrangements, they somehow did not conform to community norms of how mothers should be allocating their time. They therefore became outcasts within their own neighborhoods. Margaret, the forty-one-year-old member of Mocha Moms and mother of a seven-year-old girl described earlier, worked full time as a customer service representative in the state of Michigan for a health insurance company. While she felt comfortable in her local mothers' group, she often spent significant time in the South and would visit another type of mothers' group there. In that context, she felt as if she were a foreign presence in an environment where her work-family decisions were simply not understood.

> I got involved with [a local mothers' group] for a couple of times I came down [south]. [When I] went to [the] support group, [all the mothers] stayed at home. And to hear that I worked was kind of like, "Oh, wow. When do you have time to do this? Well, do you cook?" . . . And then, of course, when you hear, "Well, my husband gives me a five-hundred-dollar allowance a month," I'm like, "Wow." . . . I did say, "Well, you lucked out, that's good for you." And I don't know if that's just a different type of lifestyle here down south—a different mentality in the southern states—I don't know.

Notably, Margaret had a fairly confident personality and felt comfortable in her own work arrangements. Nevertheless, this sense of being alienated from her community for working was still somewhat startling to her and left her feeling unsettled.

While Margaret was resilient in the face of these judgments, social norms affected other mothers in deeply emotional ways. Some mothers who worked for pay believed that they perhaps deserved the label of being a "bad mother." They frequently reported this label as emerging from a sense of alienation that had developed once their children started attending school. Also described earlier, Diamond was forty-six, the mother of a six-year-old daughter, and a member of MomsRising. She worked as a full-time attorney at a nonprofit organization. Once her daughter was in first grade, she began to feel that, given the demands of her career, she could not measure up to other mothers in her participation in elementary school activities.

> Until now, I've seen [Mommy War attitudes] from afar but I haven't felt a part of any tension. I'm starting to feel it now that elementary school has begun because there is a disparity in school involvement that feels like both external and internal judgment. You feel more like a bad mother [when you are less involved than the other mothers]. . . . You know, [you feel different from the other] moms [who] are there volunteering at birthdays, pizza, [and] lunch.

For Diamond, these Mommy War attitudes made her think that she did not measure up to being a high-quality parent. At the same time, she felt as if she were in a double bind. No matter how hard she tried, there was no way she could both accomplish her paid work tasks effectively and meet community standards for taking proper care of her children.

For other mothers, the alienation that they experienced from their communities emerged in the form of embarrassment because paid work was not necessarily a choice. Kimberly was a thirty-six-year-old member of Mocha Moms. She had three young children, ages five, three, and one. Her husband worked in sales and she was a full-time flight attendant. Because of the poor economy, she was furloughed for several years while her children were young. These circumstances enabled her to be very hands-on in their early upbringing. Financially, however, her family experienced significant stress while she was out of the labor market, so as soon as the furloughs ended, she returned to paid work. This decision, while necessary, caused her considerable tension as she attempted to juggle her role as a paid employee and her role as a parent.

> I do think about [the fact that maybe] I'm being judged [by my working]. But I think also, for me, it's kind of like also embarrassment. I don't want [other mothers] to know that I'm still dealing with this or that issue. . . . I think, for example, just something as simple as

home management. . . . You really don't want your friends to know that, yeah, I just really have a hard time washing dishes. My dishes are always just dirty. . . . You deal with that. . . . Then, you know, you don't want to talk about things like finances because you don't want your friends going, "Oh, my gosh, she's poor. Why doesn't her husband do something? You know, he's a loser. He sucks. He should help her more." . . . You don't want that.

Like many other mothers in her situation, Kimberly felt the need to maintain appearances in her community's social circle. For her, this translated into presenting herself as a stellar housekeeper, even if she could not meet this standard. It also translated into her presenting a perfect picture of her family's financial circumstances, even if they were, in reality, under significant monetary pressure.

Aside from the feelings of embarrassment that were common among mothers who worked for pay, their feeling that they were somehow alienated from their communities gave them a strong sense of "otherness," in contrast to their stay-at-home peers. Isabella, a thirty-five-year-old mother of a son aged three, was a NAMC member. Isabella's husband was a regional manager for a restaurant chain, while she was a curriculum specialist for a public school district. This job enabled her to work full time during the school year but have her summers off. Despite having this time when she was not working, she found herself very alienated from those mothers who were at home all year.

I always feel like, you know, "I'm the working mother." And maybe they are not thinking that way, but I always feel like they are. . . . Oh, sometimes they'll say, "Oh, that's right, you are working." Like if we are doing a playdate thing . . . we might do playdates over the summer, but . . . once the end of August hits, I can't do it anymore. . . . And it's always like, "Oh, that's right, you're going to work." . . . And I don't think it's meant in a mean way, but it's like I just feel like it's kind of an us versus them [issue]. There is definitely a group of mothers that hang out all the time, you know, year round. And, of course, I'm an outsider. . . . You know, I can't do that. . . . I just think I feel like they're probably excluding me because I'm different. . . . I don't think it's meant in an intentional way. I just think that we have a very different situation where they have the ability to do stuff all year, and I'm just kind of the person who just pops in whenever I can do something.

This alienation created a lot of inner turmoil for Isabella. She commented that she was extremely jealous of her counterparts who were stay-at-home mothers, because of their lifestyle, which she was able to experience in the summers. Part of her envy, she noted, was caused by her job situation, in which she felt undervalued and underappreciated. Her boss had no tolerance for the unpredictable nature of motherhood, where children can become sick without warning; she as well as other employees were warned regularly that taking time off to attend to these issues was simply unacceptable. But another part of her envy resulted from her sense that she was trapped in a substandard lifestyle because her husband could not adequately support her.

> I often think [about] a guy that I had dated. And I'm thinking, "Oh, if I had married him, I could have been a stay-at-home mom." . . . I picked the wrong guy. [Laughter] . . . I do, I hate to admit that but I do think . . . sometimes, "I should have married for money." . . . I do, because I think in some ways . . . I'm the breadwinner in the house. . . . And there is a lot of pressure of being the breadwinner and I know that guys feel that way. . . . We always acknowledge that for a guy, "Oh, well, it's really hard being the breadwinner." But it's really hard to be the breadwinner and to be the mother. . . . You know, there is so much pressure on being a good mother, but yet I also have the pressure of being the breadwinner. . . . I feel like I have to do everything and do it well. . . . To me, there is a real conflict . . . [to] make the money and also be the good mom.

For Isabella and other mothers in this study, there were serious consequences of the alienation that they experienced from working for pay. The lack of integration with other mothers in their communities made them feel sad and, frequently, even worthless.

Mothers who work for pay are not the only lightning rods for critique in contemporary American society. Stay-at-home mothers receive their share of criticism as well. Two central themes emerged from the interviews here. First, and most commonly, stay-at-home mothers were perceived as not contributing to society, and second, they were seen as living lives of unnecessary and excessive luxury.

Anti–Stay-at-Home-Mother Judgment: Mothers as Not Contributing to Society

The first and most common judgment lodged against stay-at-home mothers was that through their choices, they were not actively enriching society. Louise, thirty-six, was a member of Mothers & More. She had one son, age three. She acknowledged that her husband, as an attorney, was the primary breadwinner in their relationship, while she, after earning her bachelor's degree, never pursued a career. Instead, she held a series of short-term jobs, in the banking industry (customer service and administrative positions) and property management (rentals and vacation planning). While she herself was satisfied in her life with this series of employment choices, she reported experiencing judgment in the form of others' believing that she was wasting her degree.

> Women will say, "Oh, gosh, you went to school and you have a degree. Why would you do something that is beneath you [like] spend time with a three-year-old all day?" To me, because I can afford to stay home, I do not need to have a job. Why would I not pass on the knowledge and the worldliness that I have gained from my education to my child? . . . Literally, he is three-years-old and he can carry on a better conversation than many adults I know. . . . I think it is really kind of a bias thing when [other moms] say that [staying at home] is beneath you. Staying home, for me, does not make me stupid.

Numerous other mothers in the study also reported that they felt judged as no longer having a "functioning brain" if they decided to stay home. Indeed, they confronted enormous pressure to demonstrate to the world that simply because they were at home did not mean that they had lost any of their intellectual capacities.

In addition to accusations of not using their intelligence, stay-at-home mothers reported experiencing a lack of acknowledgment about their very existence as valuable human beings in their own right. Marie, a thirty-three-year-old member of NAMC, had two small daughters, ages six and two. She had a bachelor's degree in science and was trained as an industrial designer; she worked on creating fabric-based products for a number of suppliers. She did this on a freelance basis, working about five to ten hours a week. Because of her flexible schedule, she considered herself to be a true stay-at-home mother. There was, however, a price to be paid for this lifestyle: invisibility. She experienced this particularly with her sister-in-law, who was employed as a school social worker and had inflexible hours. Her sister-in-law lived in the same city as her other in-laws, and unfortunately, they all shared the same attitude toward her.

> There are snide comments. . . . I want to make sure I have it worded right so as not to represent it too horribly. . . . I mean, it's a very subtle sort of thing sometimes, [but] no one ever asks me what I'm doing. No one. Mother in-law, sister in-law, brother in-law, father in-law, no one. . . . We go up there for trips. They come down here. They ask my husband, you know, How's work? How's this? No one asks me what I'm doing. . . . And if I start to tell them, then they get up and walk away. . . . Nobody even asks me about the kids. [One of my daughters] was in Daisy Scouts. I happened to be one of the leaders for her Daisy Scout troop this year. . . . [My daughter] brought out her Daisy Scout uniform [over Easter in April when we were with our in-laws]. And everybody said, "Oh, I didn't know you were in Daisy Scouts," when I had told them in September that we were doing this. So it's like . . . no acknowledgment. No questioning, like, "Oh, how's Daisy Scouts going?" You know? Nothing like that. No interest. So that's the subtle part of it, and then the more snide part is that if I do just initiate the conversation about what's going on in our lives . . . [or] in my life, my sister-in-law will say things like, "Well, not all of us have the opportunity to stay at home."

Marie and others like her coped in different ways in response to this type of treatment. For Marie in particular, religion was important. She identified her strong Catholic faith as making her feel comfortable with her decisions. Prior to getting married, she and her husband had agreed that once they had children, she would stay at home. This would enable her to give her children both a parental presence and strong religious leadership at an early age. She described her role within the home as a "moral" one and, despite others' opinions, would not be swayed to return to paid work.

Other mothers used a strategy other than religion to defend themselves against this punishment of invisibility, a strategy that placed them on the offense. With two sons ages four and one, Robin was a thirty-year-old member of Mothers & More. She had lived on the West Coast with her husband while he attended medical school and, after earning her bachelor's degree, became a social worker. She had an invigorating and important career working as a caseworker in her state's department of child protective services. In this position, she investigated allegations of abuse and would remove children and place them in foster care if the circumstances warranted it. She had her first child while working in this job. When her husband was offered a medical residency on the East Coast, the family decided to move, and after doing so, they resolved to have a second baby. At this point, they determined as a couple that she would not return to work.

> I don't know that I feel judged so much as that I want to justify to them that I am educated and I am a professional, also. Moving here [to the East Coast], I feel like when we would go to residency dinners and [other people there] would say, "What do you do?" I [would say], "Oh, I stay at home but I used to be a child welfare social worker." You want them to understand that you do not always just stay home. I do not know if it is because I really liked my job and I identified with being an accomplished person. [Maybe now] I feel like it is not a great accomplishment for me to stay home.

Robin experienced some self-doubt about her decision to be at home, and mostly it was because she felt that she did not produce concrete deliverables, such as helping others, as she had in her paid job every day. As she stated during her interview, "I had a job where I was well known, I was recognized, and I had performance evaluations but now your child [and his behavior/actions] is your new report card." Like many other stay-at-home mothers in this study, her difficulty accepting her new role led her to preempt Mommy War attitudes by describing her past employment experiences in any new social contexts in which she found herself.

Anti–Stay-at-Home-Mother Judgment:
Mothers as "Relaxing" All Day

The second most common judgment lodged against stay-at-home mothers was that they had excessive time on their hands and thus must spend most of their days simply relaxing. Cindy, a thirty-seven-year-old mother of two boys, ages six years and eighteen months, was a stay-at-home mother and a member of MomsRising. She was happy in her decision to stay at home and, in doing so, was able to provide day care for a neighbor's child while that child's parents worked for pay. This was an easy situation for her, as both her son and the neighbor's child went to school together. Yet she still felt tension at times when interacting with that mother about each of their daily schedules.

> We are not that close, but she does kind of ask, What do you do all day? types of questions. Because she never did stay home so she doesn't [really understand the concept]. She says she was home for three months because her husband had a heart attack and . . . she was like, "I was going crazy. I was so bored." It is funny to me because I don't know [what] she wants from me. [Is she is trying to get information from me] and she is not telling me, or is she just having a certain conversation? You know what I mean? . . . Yes, there are some questions that I am like, "What do you mean?" It is interesting to see the different viewpoints.

As an at-home mother of three young children and a member of Mocha Moms, Sarah, thirty-nine, felt the sting of criticism much more directly than did Cindy. Her friends who worked for pay openly teased her about being a stay-at-home mother with "clearly" an excessive amount of leisure time on her hands. Sarah did not take this criticism willingly and openly attempted to rebut it.

> Well, [my friends have] jokingly said, "Oh, you know, you're probably watching *The Young and the Restless*," and I'm like, "Well, no, I don't." I'm not able to because . . . I give them this example. Okay, you get a lunch break, you get to leave, you know, at 5:00 or whenever, when your workday is over. You get to go home. I'm at home.

I'm here 24/7. There's no time off. The only time you're off is when
the kids are asleep and you're typically still doing something. So it's
just like you can't clock out on your family.

From the perspective of stay-at-home mothers like Sarah, the work of a
stay-at-home mother never ends, and they tried to educate their friends
who work for pay about what this type of life actually entails.

While some stay-at-home mothers received vague inquiries about
what they did all day, and others received direct questioning on the
same topic (albeit in the form of teasing), still others experienced
verbal jibes that insinuated that they must have had an extravagant
lifestyle if they were able not to work for pay. More specifically, stay-
at-home mothers asserted that mothers who worked for pay often
thought of them as incredibly wealthy to be able to afford such an
arrangement. However, most stay-at-home mothers in this study remarked on the financial *sacrifices* that they had to make in order be
at home with their children. A twenty-four-year-old MOPS member,
Theresa, had a two-year-old son and a nine-month-old daughter. She
described her frustrations with being inaccurately perceived as inor-
dinately wealthy:

> Firstly, you are looked at financially like your husband can provide
> for you to stay home. [However,] although he makes a good living, we
> still sacrifice because I chose to stay at home. We cannot take fam-
> ily vacations. . . . We just chose to spend our money differently. . . .
> I do not think [people] realize what it all involves so that is why
> I think when people are just like . . . "You just stay at home," . . . they
> discount the fact that you are raising two children while you are at
> home. . . . My husband's family has had a really difficult time with my
> staying at home. . . . I am not supported. [They think] that I am just
> milking him. . . . They think it is worthless.

Theresa's feelings were common among numerous stay-at-home mothers interviewed for this study. They all described a contemporary United
States where couples valued material possessions more than the psychological, emotional, and spiritual well-being of their families. This
desire for material goods prompted both partners to enter the workforce in order to maximize the family bank account. Many stay-at-home

mothers, as they perceived themselves, chose a different route in life. They elected to forgo a higher standard of living to be at home with their children and argued that their families were richer in having stronger moral values because of this decision.

The pressures behind intensive mothering are very real. Each mother wants to do her best in giving her children the advantages they need to succeed in modern life. A central problem for the modern woman, however, is that she is pulled in multiple directions. On the one hand, engaging in intensive mothering—that is, to be a good mother—requires a commitment of time, energy, and focus. Children must be brought to their activities, they must be supervised, and they must be guided with respect to life's critical decisions. On the other hand, with the women's movement of the 1960s and 1970s, as well as with the new economic realities facing households attempting to maintain financial health, many women want to or have to work for pay. On this point, today's employment world is no less forgiving than are the cultural demands to be a good mother. Ideal workers must work hard and all the time in order to be considered dedicated to their jobs. Regardless of the arrangements mothers establish—whether working for pay or staying at home—they are likely to face criticism. There is simply no perfect choice.

The Mommy Wars in the media thus emerge, with judgments plaguing both groups of mothers. Some people argue that mothers should not be working at all, or that if they do, they no longer "fit" or "count" within their communities as good citizens. Conversely, other mothers maintain that stay-at-home mothers are not contributing to society or are simply relaxing all day. Still, as this chapter has demonstrated, the majority of mothers' group members, as reflected in both the survey and interviews, are *not* engaged in any type of judgment, either of themselves or of others. These mothers have developed a level of tolerance for others' arrangements or have lived through a series of experiences whereby they have come to understand the other mothers' perspectives in a sympathetic way. Mothers' group members, in sum, seem to know that these issues are inherently complex and are therefore quite responsive to other women's plights. This means that mothers' organizations may have little to fear by raising workplace flexibility more prominently to help alleviate some of the pressures involved in combining paid work with family responsibilities. But they need to know much more before

actively doing so: these groups must understand exactly how mothers view workplace flexibility as potentially improving their lives, and
whether there are similar views on this topic—depending on their group
affiliation, their paid work status, or both—or dissimilar ones. After all,
only with a strong consensus can these groups even consider taking the
next step in promoting national change on this critical issue.

5

Workplace Flexibility Options

It is very loud in the second-floor meeting room of a public library in a medium-size eastern city, the noise coming from twelve toddlers, all under the age of four, running around the room. At this meeting of the local NAMC chapter, eleven group members have put their chairs in a circle in preparation for the upcoming discussion. Strollers line the wall, toys litter the floor, and the kids have discovered a new game consisting of how much trouble they can cause by turning the meeting room's lights on and off.

As the mothers struggle to intervene and maintain some order, the NAMC chapter leader starts the meeting by reminding her members that they have been focusing on safety issues over the past several months. At the last meeting, they discussed how to approach the topic of "stranger danger" with their children. This month's topic is fire safety, and a local firefighter has come to answer the members' questions about keeping their families safe in the event of a fire or medical emergency. In this particular NAMC chapter, most of the mothers now stay at home, following a period when they worked for pay. Later in the meeting, several describe the stressful jobs they used to hold, which had no workplace flexibility options, making life very difficult for them. Despite such problems, they also point to the conflict they experience now that they remain at home. In their comments they reflect on the changes they have gone through.

NAMC MEMBER 1: I [used to be] a guidance counselor for over eight
hundred students living in the inner city. [I worked so hard and had
no flexibility but I loved it]. When I had a child of my own [and
left paid work], I had to rediscover who I was and the group gave
me support. I needed support in my role as a caretaker. I was lost.
I didn't know where I began and where I ended when I had kids.
When I became a mother, I became more humble.

NAMC MEMBER 2: I was an agent who represented photographers in
New York City. I was mothering my career. It brought me confidence and money. But when I had a kid, I was leaving my kid every
day [at day care and there was no way around it with my inflexible
job]. Coming to the Mothers' Center has helped me. Conflict exists with the modern family. The group is like therapy. I operated
very highly in my career. Mothering helped me realize I was too
type A. It helped me negotiate that and now [to focus my old work
energies and talents toward the idea that] my kid is my new job.
I can research this job just like I researched my new clients. My son
is my career. You are going to have bad and good days. This group
grounds me.

The two mothers at the NAMC meeting are clearly not alone in representing the complicated issues facing American families today. Both
described the rewards they experienced while working full time at
satisfying careers that they truly loved. Interestingly, however, both
noted that their jobs were extremely inflexible. There was no way to
get around the nonstop demands of their employers, co-workers, and
clients. After they had their children, through a process of careful con-
sideration, they decided to remain at home. Yet they were confused by
their new lives. In many ways they gradually adjusted, but they were
left wondering if there could have been other ways for them to combine their passion for their careers with raising their children at the
same time.

These two NAMC members chose to leave their paid jobs and, fortunately, were able to make ends meet after doing so. Many mothers who
work for pay, however, either do not want to quit or cannot do so. These
mothers face a variety of stresses in terms of the daily tasks required of
them. The bulk of the stresses have to do with these mothers' multiple
roles and how they are expected to perfectly meet the needs of these

roles. The first type of challenge relates to *role conflict*. For mothers, this conflict emerges when the demands of their paid employment directly interfere with their familial and caregiving responsibilities. Role conflict is especially difficult because there is seemingly no way out of its pressures; that is, by definition, this conundrum means that two or more sets of obligations are competing for attention during the same time block.[1]

The second issue that mothers face is *role overload*.[2] Role overload relates to the mothers' perceptions that the demands placed on them, cumulatively, are simply impossible to fulfill. Unlike role conflict, which emphasizes that stress occurs because two different sets of tasks are competing for the *same* period of time, role overload occurs when the *magnitude* of tasks is simply too overwhelming to complete *in any given time period*. As individuals struggle to execute these tasks, they may feel as if they are unable to do any of them adequately. The daily grind, then, simply becomes an exercise in frustrating futility.[3]

For mothers who work for pay and those who currently stay at home but might be searching for paid employment in the future, the pressures of role conflict and role overload can become incredibly harsh, making strategies to optimize their time management capabilities even more valuable. One resource with strong promise involves workplace flexibility policies. Flexible work arrangements, such as flexible starting and stopping times, as well as telecommuting, can help reduce role conflict and role overload by giving mothers the power to organize their days in the ways they see fit, without having to face the crunch of task overlap or pile-up. In the same way, time-off options, as well as career exit, maintenance, and reentry pathways, can help diminish both types of role stress. If mothers' family obligations become increasingly heavy, these policies give mothers the chance to focus on them exclusively, for short or long periods, without the distractions of paid employment. Put more bluntly, work tasks can be set aside until mothers are ready to resume them. In an ideal world, what types of policies would mothers in paid work and stay-at-home mothers—who may eventually wish to return to paid work—want to see implemented by businesses and organizations all across the United States? Is there any type of broad-based support for government action to encourage the development of these policies across the country? To address these questions, the survey asked all mothers—whether currently working for pay or staying at home—how important certain categories of flexibility would be to them in an "ideal job" if they were to obtain one. Their options were "very important," "somewhat important," "somewhat unimportant," and "very unimportant."

The first category of ideal flexible work arrangements included many options for mothers to consider. These pertained to flexible starting and stopping times, compressed workweeks, advance notice of overtime, advance notice of shift schedules, control over break time, part-time work, job shares, part-year work, telecommuting from home, and telecommuting from an alternative workplace. As shown in tables 5.1–5.10, mothers across groups and regardless of whether currently employed or staying at home had clear priorities in terms of such flexible work arrangements. More than 50 percent of mothers stated that flexible starting and stopping times, compressed workweeks, advance notice of overtime, advance notice of shift schedules, and the option of part-time work were "very important." Access to control over break time, job shares, part-year work, and the option of telecommuting from an alternative workplace were less important to all the mothers. The only major difference across groups and the paid work and stay-at-home divide was that the very important category of telecommuting from home garnered more than 50 percent support from Mocha Moms members, MomsRising members, and employed mothers, as well as all group mothers combined, while gaining less than 50 percent support from NAMC members, MOPS members, Mothers & More members, and stay-at-home mothers.

Time-off options and career trajectory questions were also asked of all mothers vis-à-vis their ideal jobs (tables 5.11–5.14). Here, too, we saw high levels of agreement across groups and for both employed and stay-at-home mothers. Majorities of these mothers rated short-term time off for unpredictable needs, regular time off for recurring needs, and extended time off as very important. However, assistance with re-entering the job market did not rank highly for all group mothers as a whole (46.5%) and employed mothers (42.9%) and only for a bare majority for stay-at-home mothers (51%); in addition, only a majority of Mocha Moms viewed this type of flexibility as very important, but not a large majority, at 57.1 percent (table 5.14).

TABLE 5.1.
Importance to ideal paid job: Flexible start/end times?

	All group mothers	All employed group mothers	All stay-at-home group mothers	NAMC	MomsRising	MOPS	Mocha Moms	Mothers & More
Very important	76.1	75.6	76.5	75.3	75.9	71.4	83.1	76.1
Somewhat important	20.3	20.2	20.4	20.3	20.2	24.7	13.9	20.3
Somewhat unimportant	2.6	3.2	2.0	3.3	2.8	3.1	1.8	2.6
Very unimportant	1.0	0.9	1.1	1.1	1.1	0.8	1.3	1.0

TABLE 5.2.
Importance to ideal paid job: Compressed workweek? (%)

	All group mothers	All employed group mothers	All stay-at-home group mothers	NAMC	MomsRising	MOPS	Mocha Moms	Mothers & More
Very important	76.1	75.6	76.5	75.3	75.9	71.4	83.1	76.1
Somewhat important	20.3	20.2	20.4	20.3	20.2	24.7	13.9	20.3
Somewhat unimportant	2.6	3.2	2.0	3.3	2.8	3.1	1.8	2.6
Very unimportant	1.0	0.9	1.1	1.1	1.1	0.8	1.3	1.0

TABLE 5.3.
Importance to ideal paid job: Advance notice of overtime? (%)

	All group mothers	All employed group mothers	All stay-at-home group mothers	NAMC	MomsRising	MOPS	Mocha Moms	Mothers & More
Very important	72.5	69.4	75.7	68.0	70.9	73.1	76.1	72.5
Somewhat important	19.1	20.3	17.9	24.9	20.0	19.3	15.5	19.1
Somewhat unimportant	4.8	5.4	4.2	4.4	5.2	4.9	4.4	4.8
Very unimportant	3.6	4.9	2.2	2.8	3.9	2.8	4.0	3.6

TABLE 5.4.
Importance to ideal paid job: Advance notice of shift schedules? (%)

	All group mothers	All employed group mothers	All stay-at-home group mothers	NAMC	MomsRising	MOPS	Mocha Moms	Mothers & More
Very important	79.8	76.6	83.1	77.9	81.3	86.2	79.5	79.8
Somewhat important	12.5	13.4	11.6	12.2	10.2	10.6	10.7	12.5
Somewhat unimportant	2.9	3.4	2.3	3.3	3.3	0.8	4.2	2.9
Very unimportant	4.8	6.6	2.9	6.6	5.2	2.4	5.7	4.8

TABLE 5.5.
Importance to ideal paid job: Control over break time? (%)

	All group mothers	All employed group mothers	All stay-at-home group mothers	NAMC	MomsRising	MOPS	Mocha Moms	Mothers & More
Very important	41.1	44.9	37.7	37.6	46.4	32.8	54	38.3
Somewhat important	34.6	30.5	38.8	36.5	32.3	40.3	26.7	35.5
Somewhat unimportant	17.0	16.7	17.4	19.3	13.2	21.0	13.3	17.5
Very unimportant	7.3	8.0	6.7	6.6	8.0	5.9	6.0	8.7

TABLE 5.6.
Importance to ideal paid job: Part-time work? (%)

	All group mothers	All employed group mothers	All stay-at-home group mothers	NAMC	MomsRising	MOPS	Mocha Moms	Mothers & More
Very important	65.1	64.1	66.1	70.9	55.7	68.4	57.7	65.1
Somewhat important	25.3	22.4	28.3	23.1	29.7	25.7	28.8	25.3
Somewhat unimportant	6.3	7.9	4.6	3.8	9.3	4.2	8.1	6.3
Very unimportant	3.3	5.6	1.0	2.2	5.2	1.7	5.5	3.3

TABLE 5.7.
Importance to ideal paid job: Job shares? (%)

	All group mothers	All employed group mothers	All stay-at-home group mothers	NAMC	MomsRising	MOPS	Mocha Moms	Mothers & More
Very important	27.0	24.2	30.1	33.0	26.1	27.0	29.2	27.0
Somewhat important	36.2	34.8	37.7	30.8	33.9	39.9	29.7	36.2
Somewhat unimportant	23.0	24.8	21.1	23.6	26.3	21.7	23.4	23.0
Very unimportant	13.7	16.2	11.1	12.6	13.7	11.4	17.6	13.7

TABLE 5.8.
Importance to ideal paid job: Part-year work? (%)

	All group mothers	All employed group mothers	All stay-at-home group mothers	NAMC	MomsRising	MOPS	Mocha Moms	Mothers & More
Very important	32.1	28.7	35.6	36.8	30.3	33.6	37.3	32.1
Somewhat important	35.9	33.7	38.1	35.2	36.8	40.3	31.6	35.9
Somewhat unimportant	19.7	22.1	17.2	17.0	20.5	16.2	18.2	19.7
Very unimportant	12.3	15.4	9.1	11.0	12.4	10.0	12.9	12.3

TABLE 5.9.
Importance to ideal paid job: Telecommuting from home? (%)

	All group mothers	All employed group mothers	All stay-at-home group mothers	NAMC	MomsRising	MOPS	Mocha Moms	Mothers More
Very important	51.2	54.5	47.7	49.5	52.7	43.7	66.6	47.9
Somewhat important	31.7	28.4	35.2	32.4	31.7	33.9	23.4	34.4
Somewhat unimportant	10.2	8.9	11.4	11.0	9.3	14.6	5.3	10.1
Very unimportant	6.9	8.1	5.7	7.1	6.3	7.9	4.7	7.6

TABLE 5.10.
Importance to ideal paid job: Telecommuting from alternative workplace? (%)

	All group mothers	All employed group mothers	All stay-at-home group mothers	NAMC	MomsRising	MOPS	Mocha Moms	Mothers & More
Very important	34.4	38.3	30.3	32.4	39.3	24.8	49.1	34.4
Somewhat important	32.5	30.0	35.1	30.8	32.1	32.7	29.1	32.5
Somewhat unimportant	19.4	17.6	21.3	22.5	17.6	25.7	12.6	19.4
Very unimportant	13.7	14.1	13.3	14.3	11.1	16.8	9.2	13.7

TABLE 5.11.
Importance to ideal paid job: Guaranteed short-term time off? (%)

	All group mothers	All employed group mothers	All stay-at-home group mothers	NAMC	MomsRising	MOPS	Mocha Moms	Mothers & More
Very important	86.4	86.4	86.3	87.4	87.4	85.4	89.0	86.4
Somewhat important	12.6	13.0	12.2	12.1	11.1	13.5	10.3	12.6
Somewhat unimportant	0.6	0.4	0.9	0	0.9	0.8	0.5	0.6
Very unimportant	0.4	0.2	0.5	0.5	0.7	0.3	0.2	0.4

TABLE 5.12.
Importance to ideal paid job: Guaranteed short-term time off? (%)

	All group mothers	All employed group mothers	All stay-at-home group mothers	NAMC	MomsRising	MOPS	Mocha Moms	Mothers & More
Very important	65.6	66.2	65.0	65.4	69.4	63.5	73.9	61.6
Somewhat important	27.8	27.5	28.0	27.5	25.2	30.1	21.1	30.5
Somewhat unimportant	5.6	5.4	5.9	5.5	4.6	5.1	4.0	7.1
Very unimportant	1	0.9	1.0	1.6	0.9	1.3	1.0	0.8

TABLE 5.13.
Importance to ideal paid job: Guaranteed short-term time off? (%)

	All group mothers	All employed group mothers	All stay-at-home group mothers	NAMC	MomsRising	MOPS	Mocha Moms	Mothers & More
Very important	80.5	83.0	77.8	84.1	57.4	79.3	85.9	80.5
Somewhat important	15.5	14.4	16.8	14.3	9.3	16.4	10.0	15.5
Somewhat unimportant	3.3	2.2	4.4	1.6	2.8	3.4	2.9	3.3
Very unimportant	0.7	0.4	1	0	0.4	0.9	1.1	0.7

TABLE 5.14.
Importance to ideal paid job: Guaranteed short-term time off? (%)

	All group mothers	All employed group mothers	All stay-at-home group mothers	NAMC	MomsRising	MOPS	Mocha Moms	Mothers & More
Very important	46.5	42.9	51.0	48.6	47.3	41.7	57.1	46.5
Somewhat important	33.2	32.9	33.5	33.7	30.4	39.8	26.1	33.2
Somewhat unimportant	13.5	15.9	11.0	11.6	15.0	13.6	9.2	13.5
Very unimportant	6.8	9.0	4.6	6.1	7.4	4.9	7.6	6.8

The survey data, then, indicate that across groups and across the paid-work and stay-at-home divide, most mothers would find certain components of workplace flexibility highly desirable in their ideal jobs. In other words, workplace flexibility has the potential of uniting the majority of mothers for a variety of reasons. To understand why they developed these preferences, mothers in the interviews were asked how workplace flexibility is or would be helpful to them in managing their home and work lives (table 5.15).[4] Because of the slightly different na-ture of the question (asking how flexibility is helpful to you now for mothers working for pay versus how flexibility would be helpful to you if and when you returned to paid work for mothers staying at home), the responses were thematically divided up into two sets by current paid work status. First, consider the responses of stay-at-home mothers. These mothers argued that workplace flexibility would enable them to provide their children with maximum direct care around their work schedules; facilitate their pursuit of employment opportunities of inter-est for themselves; and help them control who would take care of their children if they needed assistance, an important value for them.

Stay-at-Home Mothers: Workplace Flexibility Enables Maximum Daily Involvement with Their Children

Not surprisingly, because they were currently at home with their children, most stay-at-home mothers wanted to continue to be their children's primary caretakers if they were to pursue a paid job in the fu-ture; this was the first and most common theme reported by this group. A job with workplace flexibility would enable this to happen. Sharon, a thirty-one-year-old mother of three young children, ages five and under, and a member of Mocha Moms, explained her job requirements:

Well, I think the reason [workplace flexibility] would be very impor-tant is because, by my being at home with the children now, I am the primary caregiver. So I, of course, do all of the doctors' appointments, all of the teachers' conferences, everything. I can't foresee that chang-ing if I were to return back to work. I'm sure my husband would not have a problem with taking personal time or vacation time to help, because that's the type of person that he is. But I mean, I guess, me

TABLE 5.15.
How workplace flexibility can help mothers: Themes from the interviews (%)

	All group mothers	NAMC	Moms Rising	MOPS	Mocha Moms	Mothers & More
Stay-at-home mothers: workplace flexibility enables maximum daily involvement with their children	64.0	0.6	75.0	64.3	37.5	75.0
Stay-at-home mothers: workplace flexibility permits them to explore career opportunities	26.0	0.3	25.0	21.4	0	43.8
Stay-at-home mothers: workplace flexibility enables them to control who takes care of their children	16.0	37.5	0	7.1	12.5	18.8
Mothers who work for pay: workplace flexibility enables them to be better parents	42.7	29.4	38.1	54.5	35.3	44.4
Mothers who work for pay: workplace flexibility enables them to be better employees	17.3	11.8	42.9	45.5	17.6	33.3
Mothers who work for pay: workplace flexibility helps further women's careers	10.7	17.6	38.1	0	41.2	11.1

Note: Percentage represents working or stay-at-home mothers only in each group

being their mom, I would want to be the one [who is there for them]. If they were sick, I would want to be the one to love them and take them to the doctor. You know? [I would want to] get them home and make sure they were feeling better. I guess maybe [I feel this way] because mothers just tend to be the nurturers of the family. You know?

Janice, thirty-seven, as described earlier, echoed the sentiments expressed by Sharon. With a seven-year-old son and a two-year-old daughter, Janice was a member of MOPS. She reported that she had worked for various companies as a medical receptionist and then as a human resource trainer. During those times, work was the most important thing to her. Later, when she was laid off, she underwent a transformative experience; work came to be of secondary importance as she reevaluated her priorities.

> The clichés are all true. This time goes so fast, and it's such a critical aspect in our children's lives. . . . And [it is up to us] to build and cement this relationship we have and the memories we're going to have later when life's too busy to spend every minute together. [Right now I have] the pure enjoyment that our children get out of seeing us come into their classroom, read with them and their peers and, you know, participate in their classroom parties and things like that. It's just so critical this early time in their lives when they still want you around. . . . [I want to be there] when they ask you to [be there]. . . . I want to be the person who's holding my kid when he's sick. I don't want him to go to a neighbor's house. . . . As far as . . . having to go back to work, I would only work somewhere that allowed this type of flexibility.

Like many other stay-at-home mothers in the study, Sharon and Janice were open to returning to paid work at some point while their children were young. However, this employment would have to enable them to continue to be their children's primary caregivers first and foremost.

While Sharon and Janice focused on their responsibilities to their children in thinking about their ideal jobs, other stay-at-home mothers were more specific about the types of jobs they would and would not take, all depending on the level of interference they posed with their child care responsibilities. Joan, a MOPS member, was thirty years old and had five children, all of whom were seven and under. Her husband was a teacher and was looking into applying for an assistant principal job for the following year. Joan herself had been a teacher until the birth of her fourth child. In her interview, she discussed the possibility of returning to work, but only in a position that would suit the needs of all of her children.

> There is a company called Ten til Two or something like that that specializes in temporary or permanent positions that work around 10:00 a.m. to 2:00 p.m. or 9:00 a.m. to 1:00 p.m. [I am looking into it]. . . . Even though I am a working person and someone else's employee, I am first someone's mom. . . . I tried to stay in education, of course—that is what I wanted to do—but now I am looking for

things that would fit me even more flexibly. [Laughter]. . . . [I want something] that will fit me because now my family is expanded. . . . I will have three in school and two not in school, so the probability of someone getting sick and having to come home is even higher [than ever before]. . . . It is pretty important. We will figure it out. If it means my husband has to do more, we have to push him into it.

In the same way, Sylvia, fifty-three-years-old and a MomsRising member, was a mother of four, two of whom were under the age of eighteen (thirteen-year-old twins). She was divorced; recently her two sons had moved back in with her after a period when they had lived with their father. At the time of her interview, she was despondent because she was looking for a job but could not find one. She described her ideal job as one where she could put her children first, but she suggested how loyal an employee she was likely to be in return.

Well, because of the kind of mother I am, my kids come first and that is never going to change. So a job that lets me put my kids first [will enable me] to give my all to the job and I know that might sound stupid, but it's a fact. If I can say, "Gee, I am really sorry, I have a sick kid. I can't come in today," and I know I am not going to get fired for that or reprimanded . . . [then] I am able to focus. I am the type of person who could prioritize properly when I need to do. I would leave a sick kid in a minute and race in and get the work I needed to do and race home and be able to do the work when the kid is sleeping. . . . [Once when I was a copyeditor] there was a huge project one summer and my boss and I got our signals crossed. I thought she wanted me to do [the project] and she thought she just told me to just scope it out. She went on vacation and I literally worked twelve hours a day, seven days a week to finish that project and I did not mind a bit. And no, I didn't put in for overtime. I thought it was me doing what I needed to do for the company . . . because [the company] went the extra mile for me [in being flexible]. The [company] gave to me and I gave to [it] and it was perfect. I have a file full of glowing job recommendations.

Sylvia was married when she held this copyeditor position and reported that she refused many promotions so that she could be home with her children when they needed her. After losing this job and her marriage

falling apart, Sylvia felt stuck in a bind. She had to earn money immediately but was worried about not being available for the twins if they
required her attention. Workplace flexibility was therefore paramount
to her.

While Joan and Sylvia were emphatic about the type of job they
both desired that would enable them to continue to be central caregivers for their children, Christina, mentioned earlier, was a MOPS
member and mother of three boys aged seven, four, and two. She was
equally adamant about the type of job that she did *not* want. At age
thirty-seven, Christina was married to a civil engineer working for the
city. She had a master's degree in geology. She had worked in several
geochemistry laboratories before she had her first child and left the
workforce.

> [My] dread is to be in a career where I've got lots of demands—client
> demands—that are kind of external and my husband has a similar
> kind of job. And so, what happens if one of our kids wakes up, throw-
> ing up [laughter], and we both have an important meeting that day?
> That conflict [is real]. I've seen a lot of people bring their sick kids to
> work, and you know, the poor kid's laying there in a cubicle on the
> floor, spreading germs to everybody, and the parents, really, their full
> attention is not on their job. [Moreover,] there's not enough atten-
> tion on that poor kid. You know? So, I would say, I definitely do not
> want that scenario. . . . I want a job that—you know, especially if my
> husband continues in the job he's in—where he's got a lot of meetings
> that he doesn't have a lot of control over, and there are construction
> deadlines and things, I want to make sure that I'm in a job . . . where,
> if I've got a sick kid, I can stay home with him. . . . That would [help
> me] make the decision of whether I accept the job or not.

As a highly trained professional, Christina had experienced the demands of a job with a significant amount of pressure. In looking toward
the future, she wanted to make sure that she was able to attend to her
children's needs first, so that they could continue to obtain the proper
care that she wanted them to receive from their mother. In this way,
she knew exactly which types of jobs she wanted to avoid as she planned
the next stage of her career hunt.

Stay-at-Home Mothers: Workplace Flexibility Permits Them to Explore Greater Career Opportunities

The second most commonly reported theme regarding the benefits of workplace flexibility for currently stay-at-home mothers was that it permitted them to consider a wider breadth of employment opportunities for the future. Without flexibility, they felt somewhat restricted in their job search. Some stay-at-home mothers missed their former careers now that they were home with their children but could not stay employed because of the lack of flexibility. These mothers hoped to return to a similar field of work, but obtain a more flexible position. Recall that Robin, thirty years old and the mother of two boys, ages four and one, was a member of her local Mothers & More chapter. She loved and missed her job helping children in her state's child protective services agency; the only thing she would change in returning to this field, especially given her current family circumstances with two children, is that she would now need more flexibility. To achieve this goal, instead of being a caseworker, she wanted to seek out a position with the agency's hotline.

> I think if I were to go back to work for child welfare, I do not think I could do justice to my children, my family, or my caseload if I were doing the same job. I think if I went back, the ideal job would be to go back to the screening unit, which was the hotline. . . . I would not be able to be a lead worker if I am not there every day, but there is one job there that two people share where you work two ten-hour days. That would be fantastic. You still get all the benefits of being part time but you are only there two days a week. . . . That would be my perfect ideal job to go back to. . . . I definitely see going back to work at some point.

Julia, too, missed her job, but unlike Robin, she had had a sufficient level of workplace flexibility already in place when she left. This experience made her even more insistent that she would seek out workplace flexibility in her next position. A member of Mothers & More, Julia, age thirty-five, had two young boys, ages three years and eight months. While she was earning her master's degree in history, Julia worked as an editor at a legal magazine. She cherished this employment opportunity, especially since her supervisors treated her with the dignity and respect she believed workplace flexibility helps create in all employment environments.

> Being a mom and raising kids is a complicated, unpredictable process. . . . In my previous job, they gave me a lot of flexibility when I was pregnant and actually with my first child when I was on bed rest. I was allowed to work from home. It was like I knew that they trusted [me] and I could set my own hours. I could work as I [wanted to] and my bosses trusted that I was going to do the job. When you get to places where there is a strict schedule, [I] almost feel like I have to clock in and out because [the bosses] want to micromanage me. Does that make sense? . . . [At my job, they understood] that my family is a priority. It is not that my family would be more of a priority than my job; it is just that sometimes you only can get a doctor's appointment at a certain time, so that flexibility gives a woman confidence. Then, [for me, I] feel like [I] can do [my] job better and just [have] more job satisfaction. Somebody is not sitting there looking at the watch [and questioning you,] "Were you only gone one hour and a half to take your kid to the doctor?" They know that you are going to do what you need to for your family, and then come back and also get your job done.

Julia was fortunate in that her husband had a job providing security for the navy, and the family could live comfortably on his paycheck for the time being. In the meantime, she was experimenting with another flexible career on her own: floral arranging for formal engagements. If this business took off, she could look forward to a new career in which she had complete control over her hours.

Still other stay-at-home mothers cited flexibility as necessary for them because of the difficult demands of their husbands' employment. A member of MOPS, Jane, thirty-seven, was a mother of a six-year-old girl and a three-year-old boy. She had spent years in school working toward her PhD in French. While studying for her degree, she was employed as a teaching assistant at her university and also worked as a private tutor. She left the paid labor force when it was too difficult for her to manage both her children and her career. This was primarily because her husband's career as a pediatrician came first. He earned more money in the household by far, so they decided as a couple that any employment pursuit of hers would first need to accommodate his schedule.

> People always ask me, "Are you going to go back to work?" Yes, that will be wonderful, but my husband's job is still very demanding. Someone has to be there to pick up the kids from school. Somebody has to be able to be with them during the summertime. I just cannot take a job that I would want to. I would have to have something flexible to still maintain that role of primary caretaker. Just because the children get into school, it is not over. . . . The other thing is my husband's job is not flexible. I can see in some couples, [it] might work to say, "Hey, you pick up the slack this week and I will pick up the slack next week." Well, he cannot do that. It is not that he is not willing. Children are always sick. People are always having babies. His job [as a pediatrician] does not have a lot of flexibility built into it. If I would go back to work, I would have to be the one who would be flexible. . . . I have thought about it because I did put so much time into my education. I did not pursue a PhD in French with the end result in not having a job. I just love that discipline of study and the goal for me was the degree. I feel like I reached that goal; however, it would be nice to use it.

Highly educated, Jane wanted a chance to use her degree to the fullest. She truly desired to return to the paid labor market, through formally teaching French at a university, teaching French through private tutorial sessions, or working as she had before in helping to organize international conferences at her local university. The constraints of her husband's job convinced her, however, that only those positions with maximum flexibility would work for her and her family.

Esmeralda was in a somewhat more dire situation than Jane's. Her workplace flexibility concerns also revolved around her husband, but in her case she was facing an immediate threat to her family's finances. At age forty-five, she had a four-year-old girl and a two-year-old boy. She was currently a member of Mothers & More. While she had pursued some graduate school, Esmeralda never believed that she had developed a true career. Throughout her life, she had bounced from opportunity to opportunity, from waiting tables, to teaching English in the inner city, to ultimately entering the information technology (IT) world. In the field of IT, she started to develop strong analytical writing skills. Once she had her children, however, she elected to leave the paid labor force to take care of them. When the Great Recession of 2008 hit, Esmeralda started reevaluating her decisions. Her husband, who worked in IT as well, lost his job, and Esmeralda started to panic.

> The longer I'm not working and the longer I [am] out of the work-force, it leaves me in a vulnerable position. . . . And that makes me uncomfortable. . . . [When] I was single or even just the two of us, if I didn't make enough money, I went out and got a second job. . . . I waited tables on weekends. When I was teaching, I waited tables on weekends because I didn't make enough money. [This summer when my husband lost his job], I felt so vulnerable and trapped. . . . He was trying to find a job so [it] didn't make sense for me to go get some job because what if he did get a job? He can make way more money than me. . . . And I already had kind of had it in the back of my mind like, gosh, if anything ever happened to him or happened [to us], you know, [if] our marriage fell apart, I'm pretty vulnerable here. It really brought it to a head this summer with seeing how trapped I felt; like, oh my God, I can't just like go get a job.

By assessing her own experiences, Esmeralda concluded that with more workplace flexibility options at her disposal, she would be able to re-enter the workforce and keep her skill set current. This would diminish the exposure that she felt to the ups and downs of her husband's career.

Stay-at-Home Mothers: Workplace Flexibility Enables Them to Control Who Cares for Their Children

The third most common theme among stay-at-home mothers of why workplace flexibility might be important to them as they consider a return to the paid labor market was that it would enable them to most effectively select others to take care of their children when necessary. For some mothers, this was partly a cost issue: paying someone outside the family to take care of their children simply did not make financial sense. Pamela, forty-two years old and the mother to two boys, ages eight and two, was a member of NAMC. At the beginning of the previous year, she and her husband had switched her older son from public school to private school. Given the high cost of tuition, she decided that she needed to go back to work and was seeking an entry-level retail job.

> Well, I am in the [job] application process. The jobs that I am looking for are in the evenings or weekends because I want my husband to be able to take care of the children rather than to pay somebody. . . . And that would be the times when he would be available to do that.

As Pamela later noted, part of her decision to look for flexible work had to do with child care costs; it was simply cheaper for her husband to care for the children than it would be to hire an individual outside the family. Beyond this, a critical component of her choice was that she preferred that her husband take care of the children rather than anyone else. She trusted him more than any outsider to make the best decisions about their well-being.

This latter point was a common theme among stay-at-home mothers in this study; they preferred flexible work because it gave them more control over who would be their children's caregivers even when cost was not an issue. Emily, referred to earlier, was a thirty-five-year-old mother of two boys, ages three and five, and belonged to Mothers & More. One of the benefits of her organization was that it provided child care exchanges, that is, if a mother needed someone to care for her children while she attended to an appointment or otherwise needed time for herself, she could call on the group for assistance in finding someone to look after her children. For Emily, though, this was not a sufficient arrangement as she looked for more regular, part-time work.

> You know, obviously, having kids, you have to pick them up because they only do preschool [from] 9:00 a.m. to 11:30 a.m. There are all these chunks of time where, if you had a flexible schedule, it would be a lot easier to manage or even a workplace where you can bring your kids where they have child care. One of the biggest reasons I have not gone back to work is because I do not feel I have a good option of who would take care of my kids. I cannot get a nanny because I do not really need full-time work. My parents do not live close. I do not really

want a fifteen-year-old babysitter. The college kids are great, in the summer, but then they go back to school. It is hard.

Having other options, such as flexible work arrangements, would clearly help mothers like Emily reenter the paid labor market while being comfortable with the care arrangements she would then be able to make for her children. As a trained speech pathologist, Emily was in high demand. She could choose to work in private practice, in a school setting, or in a hospital. However, to pursue these opportunities, she needed to know that she could obtain solid child care coverage for the limited hours she wanted to work. Unfortunately, at the time of her interview for a potential position, Emily remained unable to move forward in planning the next stages of her career, as she was unable to patch together a suitable system of supervision for her children.

As these interviews demonstrate, stay-at-home mothers clearly thought about workplace flexibility options as they decided whether they were going to return to paid work. Mothers who currently worked for pay also valued flexibility, albeit for somewhat different reasons. The most common themes that emerged among this latter set of mothers was that flexibility would enable them to be better parents, feel as if they were more dedicated employees, and sense that they were being treated with more respect by their employers.

Mothers Who Work for Pay: Workplace Flexibility Enables Them to Be Better Parents

For mothers who work for pay, workplace flexibility was a central motivating feature in organizing their lives in their current jobs or as they remained open to new jobs that might come their way and provide them with opportunities for advancement. Most important, according to these mothers, workplace flexibility enabled them to be the best parents they could be, which was of critical value to them and the first and most common theme reported among this group.

Some mothers deliberately chose careers that would provide them with flexibility so they could spend the maximum amount of time with their children. Evelyn, thirty-nine and the mother of two girls, ages six and three, was a member of her local MOPS chapter. In her interview, she recalled having known what she wanted to be—a physical therapist—by the time she was in the third grade. This career, while demanding, brought with it many privileges, including flexibility.

> I knew as I got older that being a physical therapist would allow me flexibility in life. . . . [I have always wanted] to have a family and to do the things that I wanted to be able to do. . . . And so I do have a ton of flexibility and, yeah, because of that I can organize my life around work. . . . I just got off the phone with one of my girlfriends earlier today who is in a business [where] she may or may not have a job in November because her company was bought out by another one. . . . [You know], she's not going to have that kind of flexibility in finding a [new] job, and she will have to maybe work for an employer who expects her to prove herself by maybe working extra hours and things like that. . . . I've chosen to not work in a field that requires me to be married to it.

Similar to other mothers in the study, Evelyn deliberately sought out a career where she knew that she would have the most time to dedicate to her family. She received satisfaction from her job but at the same time, and more important, devoted herself to her children's needs. While Evelyn knew that she wanted to pursue physical therapy at a young age, other mothers, such as Judith, deliberately changed their career course in order to obtain similar levels of workplace flexibility. For Judith, a member of MOPS, twenty-five years old, and the mother of two boys, three years old and 6 months, this decision was primarily motivated by her desire to avoid day care. Although she had earned her bachelor's degree in the field of education, once she had her first child, she decided to work on an on-call basis doing hospital emergency room admissions. In this position, she could control which assignments she would take. Moreover, to minimize the need to rely on anyone but her husband to care for the children, she accepted these hospital assignments only on the weekends.

> It is very important for me regardless of my education . . . to have a job where, even if I had to work, my kids are at their parents' [house]. I am uncomfortable with the idea [of paying] for someone to watch my children. . . . My job right now, even though I may have an entry-level

position, is basically the only kind of job I can have . . . until my kids
are school age when I can venture out to do something else. . . . Right
now I want my commitment to be with my young children and later
on when they do not need me so much or when they are in school,
then I may look for other things [to which] maybe I can commit myself. . . . I grew up with a single mother and I have a sister. We were
both in day care. I always grew up feeling that my mother was always
so tired all the time and so cranky—just always feeling overwhelmed
and not happy. When I had my son, I fell in love with him and just
wanted to give him everything that I could.

Judith went on to describe how she hoped her children would have a
different relationship from the one she had had with her mother; she
never wanted them to feel as if she did not have the emotional resources
to satisfy their demands. Indeed, her own negative childhood memories
were so strong that even though she worked on an on-call basis, and
only on weekends, she still worried that these employment obligations
were preventing her from adequately meeting her responsibilities toward her children's needs.

Other mothers did not necessarily seek out careers with high degrees
of flexibility, but once they were exposed to it in their jobs, they could
not imagine life without such options. Stephanie was a thirty-four-year-
old mother of two young boys, ages four years and thirteen months. She
also was a member of NAMC. After graduating college with a bachelor's
degree and putting some work toward earning a master's, Stephanie
began full-time employment in the biotechnology and pharmaceutical
industries. She worked in the field of quality auditing, making sure that
companies were adhering to their contractual agreements. After she
had her sons, she became an independent contractor, producing technical writing in the same professional arenas, on a part-time basis. She
quickly discovered that this was an ideal arrangement, allowing her to
manage her work and home life.

I absolutely value the flexibility. I would say it is probably the best
feature of the job that I have. . . . You know, well, with children, everything is up in the air all the time. You never know when someone
is going to take a spill and need to go to the doctor's or pick up a cold.
I mean kids are constantly picking up viruses here and there. You

know, additionally, my husband has a huge extended family here so it's really valuable to me to be able to be flexible and lend a hand if any of them need help with anything. And frankly, I think for my own personal sanity, now that I've been in this position for two and a half [years] and I have so much flexibility in my life, I realize what an asset it is to be able to, you know, get up from my computer and go to the school. . . . Or you know, get up from my computer, and I don't know, take the car to the shop if something is wrong with it. [I do not] have to schedule [time off] with someone to get that done, and it's just amazingly easy to get [things] done. And you know, my primary clients are very easygoing. . . . I [can] say to them, you know, yes, I can do this, [but] I probably won't be able to get to you until 11:00 p.m. If it's not a problem with you that I work on this project outside of standard work hours, I'm happy to take this on. And I would say that 99 percent of the time, they're fine with that.

Just as Stephanie reduced her hours and ultimately found flexibility to be the most satisfying feature of her job, Dawn, too, discovered the value of flexibility only once she had children. A MomsRising member and mother of two children under the age of four, Dawn worked in the field of software development and testing for over ten years and for three different companies. In her current position, at the age of thirty-two, she had to work forty hours a week, but she could alter her start and finish times if she had to attend to her children's needs. In addition, she had the option of working at home if one of her children needed her for any reason during the day.

Before I had kids, I really did not care either way if I could work from home or not. With my first position [in the software testing industry, the bosses had] that available but I never took advantage of it. I did not need to. However, with the [second] company I worked for . . . being able to work from home was necessary because . . . we were called upon during odd hours [to complete work tasks] when we were not typically in the office. . . . It just so happened to be that it was helpful, once you did have kids, to be able to [continue to work at home if you needed it and I have it in my third job as well]. Now that I do have a family, it would most definitely be something that I would make sure I had in my next job or any future jobs.

Notably, both Stephanie and Dawn stated that they had not been familiar with the benefits of workplace flexibility prior to having children. Once they experienced the demands of motherhood, however, they quickly became devoted adherents of this approach to organizing their employment lives. In other words, having children, made them flexibility converts.

Other mothers tried to return to work after the birth of their children but then determined that they needed flexibility if they were going to maintain any type of paid labor force participation. Ellen was described earlier as a thirty-nine-year-old mother of two daughters, four and two, and a member of MomsRising. As a computer science specialist who loved her job, she had planned to return to her regular position with traditional hours once she had her first baby. However, she quickly discovered that this arrangement would not work for her.

[Once I had my first child, I had to say to my employers,] "I can't work full time. I can't. It's not possible." [I was just so happy when they said], "Well, we think that we could work with you about that." I think that I've engineered my life really to have a flexible work situation always. It's really important for me to pick up my kids from preschool. We can have somebody else do it, and that wouldn't be that hard, but to be in touch with their teachers and to hear about their day [is really important to me]. When I work at home, we have a nanny with the kids . . . but I can kind of hear the rhythm of their day. I can stop and have lunch with them or help the nanny if [any] child seems to be having a total meltdown. That's really, really, really, very important.

Ellen reported that she was extremely satisfied that her employer accommodated her request to work at home. Interestingly, what also made her happy in balancing work and family was that her husband's job was extremely flexible as well. When Ellen had a deadline or other pressing work obligation, she relied heavily on her partner to share child care duties with her. In fact, she was one of the few mothers in the study who reported that it was this combination of assistance—workplace flexibility *and* her husband's contributions—that made her life more manageable.

Mothers Who Work for Pay: Workplace Flexibility Enables Them to Be Better Employees

The second most common theme regarding why mothers who worked for pay valued flexibility was that it made them better employees. Mothers defined *better* in different ways. Tiffany, a twenty-eight-year-old MomsRising member and the mother of an eleven-month-old daughter, defined a better employee as one who was simply happier. Tiffany worked full time as a greenhouse manager at a nonprofit research organization.

> [I work at] a very flexible [organization], I guess you would say. Like today, I had to get new tires on my car so I was two hours late. No one said anything because they know that I manage my time and I get things done when they need to be done. They know that I came in and checked on the plants before I went into town. It is a very nice environment and very family oriented, and so they understand that I have a little one at home. . . . I can't even put a value on it. It is great. If my daughter is sick and I need to take her to the doctor's, there are no questions asked. I just say, "Hey, I need to go," and they say, "Okay, we'll see you later." . . . I think [flexibility] is very helpful to employers; they have happier employees. If I were here, but I knew that my daughter had to go to the doctor but I could not take her, I would not do nearly as well of a job as I would if I could just take her and then come back and work. So I think it would be a tremendous benefit to employers.

Tiffany maintained that her overall level of satisfaction with her job was much higher with workplace flexibility. She also noted that employers receive another benefit when they are flexible with mothers like herself. She indicated that she was willing to accept a lower wage in exchange for favorable work-related options, and if her feelings were indicative of those of other mothers, employers could be gaining financially as well from providing flexibility.

Other mothers argued that being a parent was important to them, but so was maintaining a strong foothold in the working world. They mentioned that their employers benefited in many ways beyond reduced payrolls. Rachel was identified earlier as a thirty-five-year-old member of Mothers & More. She had a three-year-old son and was expecting another child shortly. Trained in the field of computer consulting, she had worked for pay her entire adult life and had earned a graduate degree. When she had her first child, she was looking for flexibility and soon found a job as a systems analyst where she could work full time from home.

> [Flexibility] is extremely important to me. I like to say that I get the best of both worlds really. I get to be at home and be around my family. I am here whenever they need me, in case of an emergency or something like that, but I still get to keep the work identity that I acquired before being a mom. . . . When he is sick, I can pick him up from school and take him to appointments, and still do all of those roles or those things that we see that moms are supposed to do, along with still being able to be in the workforce. [I love having] that work identity. That is really important to me. . . . Not that there is anything wrong with [staying at home]. I have a great appreciation for stay-at-home moms. It is just for me—I did not want to just be that.

Because Rachel's ability to retain her work identity made her feel so empowered, she took extraordinary steps to make her employer satisfied. She reported rising early every morning to get work accomplished before her son got up. This earlier schedule also enabled her to be in tune with the working rhythms of her East Coast office and meet their needs on a real-time basis (she lived in a western region of the country). Similarly, Mothers & More member Sara, thirty-four years old and the mother of two children, ages four and one, described her relationship with her employer as one built on gratitude that ultimately generated strong dedication on her part. As a freelance writer, she felt the effects of the economic recession of 2008 strongly. With her husband working in the declining newspaper business, she feared that he would lose his job and that the entire family would need to move back to her home state of Minnesota, where he could work for her father. She also recognized that she wanted to return to work, but not at the expense of taking care of her children. Fortuitously, while attending one of her children's friend's birthday parties, she met another woman who seemed be working at an ideal company for a mother like her. The firm was hiring; she learned that she could be employed as a senior writer at this communications company four days a week for a total of thirty-two hours.

> I told my boss the first month into working there . . . that with this nice entry into going back into work, "You are making so many lives better." There is a different dynamic between my husband and me. We are not quarreling and stressed. I used to hammer him about finding a plan B. He still needs to find a plan B. He still needs to figure out what he is going to do if he is laid off, but I feel like [now] we have a safety net. My kids, I think, can feel [the difference]. Even if we did not argue in front of them, there is less tension in the home. . . . Just in general, I am just a different person than I was back in the summer or the fall of 2008. I felt really hopeless [then]. I thought I did not feel any trust in my ability to get independent contracting work, considering the economy, and I landed at this company that just understood that I was willing to work my tail off, in gratitude, because they are giving me this understanding that I have never received before in my field. . . . It has really made my husband, my children, and my life much better to have this nice understanding, flexible job. . . . I was driving home once and I kind of got choked up about it. I said, "I love my job." I realize this and you know, the company has a super worker in me. I just think, today is my technical day off and I checked my work e-mail and something came up. It was a telephone call that came during naptime and I was like, I can swing this. They have given me so much; I can swing listening to a phone call for fifteen minutes during my kid's naptime. I can do that.

Sara was especially grateful and willing to go the extra step for her employer because she knew that in her industry, having such flexibility was rare. Before she had children, she described her experience working for the Associated Press as incredibly demanding and stressful. She regularly worked fifteen-hour days and, according to her, was simply expected to do so. Parents who had to leave at 5:00 p.m. to pick up their children were looked down on and she quickly realized that she would never advance if she were to follow in their footsteps. According to Sara, "In fact, I remember [my employers at the AP] saying, 'You have to decide whether you are a journalist or a parent.'" With this as the company's philosophy, Sara knew she had to make a change.

Clearly, employers benefit when their employees are generally happier and more dedicated (usually prompted by gratitude). But some mothers went a step further by arguing that employers, when they offer flexibility, gain something more important—even if it can seem intangible—that will benefit all employers in the long run: they ultimately help produce a new generation of loyal citizen-workers. Katherine, forty-three and the mother of a nine-year-old girl and a four-year-old boy, was a member of MOPS. For years Katherine had worked as a high school history teacher, often spending most of her after-school hours planning lessons for the next day, as well as leading numerous extracurricular activities. Because one of her children had special needs, Katherine requested time off during her workday for her child's appointments, but she found such accommodations difficult to obtain. Unfortunately for her, her supervisors argued that they simply could not cover her classroom as requested. The barriers raised by her employers ultimately forced her to transfer to the more flexible profession of nursing. She described her philosophy of how employers could reap the benefits of flexibility by taking a broader approach to their operations, taking into account the context of the wider society. If her employers had viewed flexibility through this prism, she asserted, she would not necessarily have faced a disruption in her career.

> Yes, I realize, Mr. Employer, that it is inconvenient to have someone take off to go to a field trip, a parent-teacher conference, a discipline hearing, or take a kid to see a therapist, or a speech therapist, whatever the reason is. I realize that there is an inconvenience to the employer but, in the end, kids who have that kind of attentive parents and participatory parents tend to be more participatory and better adults. . . . While the employer is suffering some inconvenience in the short term by having a parent . . . out of the office, [there are long-term benefits]. In the long run, employers are going to get new employees that are better people.

Critically, while Katherine noted the importance of flexibility and how it could help employers provide the best opportunities for an engaged workforce, she also noted that this was a two-way responsibility. That is, like other mothers in the study, she pointed out that mothers never should abuse these policies, since the majority of employers still have an obligation to make a profit.

Mothers Who Work for Pay: Workplace Flexibility Helps Further Women's Careers

The third most common theme related to the importance of workplace flexibility for mothers currently working for pay was that overall, it helps women along in furthering their career trajectory. Mothers' group members in the study noted that women often have to leave their jobs or assume less prestigious ones once they have children in order to survive in the work world. Elizabeth, fifty-two years old and with a twelve-year-old daughter and a nineteen-year-old son, was a member of MomsRising. A computer software entrepreneur and a political activist, she recognized that women face challenges that rarely confront men:

> I think that the bias against people who have taken off substantial time is unnecessary and bad for everybody because fundamentally, one of the reasons why we don't have as many women in leadership as I think we should is [a woman comes in] and [she is] on the mommy track. [Mothers are put in these second-tier jobs]. The fact is that women and mothers specifically bring certain insights to the table and I want them in leadership. I want them as people helping make the decisions and yet they are dramatically underrepresented if you look at the Fortune 500. It's just shocking how few women are there. And I bet if you checked into how many [of the women] were mothers, it would be disproportionately those who were not.

Echoing these sentiments, Paula, mentioned earlier, thirty-nine years old and the mother of a seven-year-old boy, was a member of Mothers & More. After working in various administrative positions, she ultimately found a job with a national bookstore chain as part of its creative team. Because her husband had been out of work for a period of time, she had to work full time. While she enjoyed her job, it was difficult to manage, because her son had developmental delays and needed various types of therapy. She described losing an opportunity for promotion that she had once had within her sights because her company was unwilling to provide flexible work options so that she could meet her son's needs.

> I actually had the opportunity and was encouraged to put in for a manager's position that opened up for our group actually. Our director wanted me to put in for it, but the work environment at [my company] is really intense, and with my son's needs, I just did not think I could handle both [the caregiving and the job]. I really did not and as it is, I put in more hours than I want to. I cannot imagine if I had a higher level of responsibility. . . . I declined and she understood but I was frustrated because I would enjoy that position if the circumstances were different. . . . Even if it were not such a long commute, I might have been able to make it work. . . . I do not see any reason why I should not be able to work, doing the job that I do, from home, at least part of the week. More flexibility would actually free me up to take on a higher level of responsibility. I think it is critical to job satisfaction. I think it is critical to retention.

Paula later explained that one of her colleagues was in a senior manager role at the same company, but recently had her third baby. This colleague explained that she, too, felt that she was being forced to choose between work and her family, because, again, the bookstore offered no flexibility. Since her colleague's husband earned a decent living, she was able to quit in order to stay at home, even though this was not her preferred option. Paula viewed this as a tragic loss of talent and a decision that other mothers should not be forced to make.

Should There Be a Government Role in Promoting Flexibility?

Both stay-at-home mothers and mothers currently working for pay expressed a number of reasons for how and why workplace flexibility could help them now or in the future better manage their work-family lives. They all clearly argued that such options were fundamental to their success as caregivers and workers. How, though, would they encourage businesses and other organizations to implement the workplace changes that they so strongly desire? What do they believe the role of government should be in promoting flexibility? Can there be agreement across mothers' groups, as well as between mothers who currently work for pay and mothers who stay at home?

Both the survey and the interviews provide answers to these questions. In the survey, respondents were presented with a series of four statements, each representing a particular view of the role of government in promoting flexibility, and then were asked if they agreed or disagreed with the statements. The statements described conditions ranging from a minimal level of government intervention to a much higher level of intervention. The first statement, reflecting the most minimal level of intervention, was "The government should educate employers and employees about the benefits of flexible work arrangements and best practices regarding how to implement flexible work arrangements." As shown in table 5.16, of all group mothers, 83.4 percent agreed, with only 16.6 percent disagreeing. Support was also high across groups; these values ranged from 67.4 percent for MOPS members to 92.9 percent for MomsRising members. When these numbers were broken down by paid work status, there was also significant agreement. A full 85.4 percent of mothers currently working for pay and 81.2 percent of stay-at-home mothers agreed. Clearly, education about flexibility is an area where substantial consensus among mothers from all backgrounds is strong.

The next statement represented a slightly stronger version of government intervention in workplace flexibility policy: "The government should encourage employers to voluntarily increase access to flexible work arrangements, by, for example, providing grants, awards, and tax incentives." Interestingly, as table 5.17 shows, support stayed constant, with 82.9 percent of all group mothers agreeing, and only 17.1 percent disagreeing. The range by group was 66.7 percent for MOPS members to 93 percent for MomsRising members, demonstrating once again that this is an issue around which the majority of mothers can rally. Support also remained high across both mothers working for pay (86%) and staying at home (79.5%).

The last two survey statements involved "requiring" the government to become involved in promoting flexibility; these were the strongest assertions presented to the mothers (tables 5.18–5.19). More specifically, the survey asked mothers to respond to the following statements: "The government should *require* employers to establish a process under which employees can request flexible work arrangements and

TABLE 5.16.
Agreement: Government should educate employers regarding flexible work (%)

	All group mothers	All employed group mothers	All stay-at-home group mothers	NAMC	MomsRising	MOPS	Mocha Moms	Mothers & More
Agree	83.4	85.4	81.2	91.1	92.9	67.4	83.4	85.4
Disagree	16.6	14.6	18.8	8.9	7.1	32.6	16.6	14.6

TABLE 5.17.
Agreement: Government should encourage employers regarding flexible work (%)

	All group mothers	All employed group mothers	All stay-at-home group mothers	NAMC	MomsRising	MOPS	Mocha Moms	Mothers & More
Agree	82.9	86	79.5	90.7	93	66.7	82.9	86
Disagree	17.1	14	20.5	9.3	7	33.3	17.1	14

TABLE 5.18.
Agreement: Government should require employers to establish a flexible work process (%)

	All group mothers	All employed group mothers	All stay-at-home group mothers	NAMC	MomsRising	MOPS	Mocha Moms	Mothers & More
Agree	59.2	63.7	54.4	72.2	74	41.5	59.2	63.7
Disagree	40.8	36.3	44.6	27.8	26	58.5	40.8	36.3

TABLE 5.19.
Agreement: Government should require employers to grant some flexible work (%)

	All group mothers	All employed group mothers	All stay-at-home group mothers	NAMC	MomsRising	MOPS	Mocha Moms	Mothers & More
Agree	45.9	50	41.5	57	62.2	30.5	60.6	40.6
Disagree	54.1	50	58.5	43	37.8	69.5	39.4	59.4

employers must consider those requests" and "The government should *require* employers to grant a certain number of requests for flexible work arrangements per year." With the addition of this "requirement" language, support was lower for both these initiatives; however, compellingly, the majority of mothers agreed with establishing a process to request flexibility, at 59.2 percent. At the individual group level, support was much more fluid, ranging from 41.5 percent of MOPS members to 74 percent of MomsRising members. However, more than half of both mothers currently working for pay and those staying at home also agreed, at 63.7 percent and 54.4 percent, respectively. It was only the last statement, which would require that employers actually grant a certain number of flexible work arrangements per year, that lost majority support, with only 45.9 percent of all group mothers agreeing. At the individual group level, support ranged from 30.5 percent of MOPS members to 62.2 percent of MomsRising members. In addition, about 50 percent of mothers working for pay concurred, while only about 41.5 percent of mothers staying at home registered support.

Overall, then, there is widespread agreement among all group mothers—and among both mothers working for pay and mothers staying at home—that the government should play some role in promoting workplace flexibility. Championing voluntary educational and financing initiatives, such as awarding grants, awards, and tax incentives for businesses and other organizations, proved to be the most popular options, with support across the board from the majority of mothers. Measures that would set up requirements for businesses were less popular, but still garnered approximately 50 percent approval levels among selected groups of mothers. To provide additional meaning to these survey data, all mothers in the in-depth interviews were asked about the role, if any, the government should play in helping to encourage workplace flexibility. More specifically, they were asked, "Some people say that the government should promote workplace flexibility, either through education, tax breaks, or laws. Other people say that the government should not be involved at all and employers should do this only if they want to. What do you think? Is this more the job of the government or employers?"

In this discussion, the views of both mothers who work for pay and stay-at-home mothers are analyzed together, as there was substantial overlap in themes (table 5.20). In explaining their responses, the

TABLE 5.20.
Attitudes toward the government's role in promoting workplace flexibility: Themes from the interviews (%)

	All group mothers	NAMC	Moms Rising	MOPS	Mocha Moms	Mothers & More
Supportive of a government role in promoting flexibility: unique institution to force change	21.6	28	28	12	28	12
Supportive of a government role in promoting flexibility: necessity of prodding the private sector	12.8	20	8	16	16	4
Against a governmental role in promoting flexibility: preference for business autonomy	12.0	8	12	8	20	12
Mixed view: values business autonomy but sees benefits for workers	12.0	12	4	8	12	24

mothers who agreed with a strong role for the government maintained that it is a unique institution that can bring about welcome change and that the private sector needs prodding in introducing new business models into its long range plans. On the other hand, a smaller set of mothers disagreed with a governmental role in this area, mostly because they believed businesses should have an autonomous role in determining their own affairs. And last, some mothers reported a mixed view on this topic; these mothers wanted to protect businesses' right to self-determination but, at the same time, asked them to consider providing workers with more opportunities to control their work-family lives.

Supportive of a Government Role in Promoting Flexibility: Unique Institution and Necessity of Prodding the Private Sector

There were two central justifications that respondents gave for supporting a government role in promoting workplace flexibility. First and most commonly, they noted that as an institution the government was in a unique position to promote social change and, second, they saw a necessity for government to at times prod the private sector so that businesses would ultimately see that it was in their interest in the long run to support flexibility options.

Many interview respondents argued that the government has a special place in American life as a mobilizer of societal innovation, and therefore it should do whatever is necessary to advance workplace flexibility options as part of its leadership role. For Tina, thirty-four and a Mothers & More member, the government must push for reform in this area because it is not part of American culture to foster these types of novel work arrangements organically.

> I think the government can set a good tone. It is all well and good to say that a corporation might do it on its own, but I just think that that is not really our culture. With it not being our culture, then it helps to have the government . . . setting forth those changes, if you will. . . . If you had something mandating that a certain amount of flexibility were required, that would help a tremendous amount. I do not think we are going to get there without that.

The mother of a two-year-old daughter and a five-month-old son, Tina maintained that government intervention would be the only way to turn expectations around regarding mothers and their work needs. Simply put, employers have to understand that mothers require time to work and to care. But later in her interview, Tina also noted that even with this push, American society would not change overnight; the government would have to be a consistent propellant behind this workplace change that could take generations to realize.

From a somewhat different perspective, Diamond, forty-three and a MomsRising member, made the case that workplace flexibility advances the well-being of the country and therefore the government should be actively involved. Not only would such policies help her personally raise her own daughter but also others would benefit from her having these options.

> It is in the country's interest for people to have children. And [it is also] in the country's interest for those children to be well cared for,

to get the best possible early childhood care, and to be safe, supported, and secure. [It is in] our interest ranging from the economic point of view to crime [prevention] to any other number of things. . . . It benefits everyone in the country, both people with and without children.

Workplace flexibility, Diamond argued, was a quantifiable good that did much more than simply provide hope to her own particular family. In her case, she was able to convert her high-profile legal career in the private sector, where she had worked over eighty hours a week, to a position in the nonprofit sector, where she had a more manageable schedule. As she pointed out in her interview, if available to all workers, the changes that she was able to make would offer broader societal benefits for all Americans. Children would receive more attention and grow up to be healthier and more productive adults. Therefore, as a unique institution, the government should invest in these policies for the well-being and prosperity of its citizenry across the nation.

The second major reason that mothers gave in favor of government intervention was that without such intervention, employers on their own would not take on the risk of initiating this type of workplace initiative. According to this view, although research has documented the many benefits of workplace flexibility, many employers are hesitant to experiment with change in their labor force practices. If the government provided a functional model of such arrangements or otherwise subsidized their introduction, perhaps employers' fears would be eased. In the interviews, mothers emphasized how employers could benefit if the government pushed them in the right direction. Some mothers stressed productivity gains for employers. Raven was a thirty-four-year-old NAMC member and mother of two young girls, one age three years and the other nine months. Although she currently was a stay-at-home mother, she had previously worked in television production. After she had her first daughter, she knew that she wanted to work fewer hours, and she tried to think creatively about how to do this, given the demands of her job. A woman she knew also had recently delivered a baby, and she decided she would set up a meeting with that new mother to discuss their options. They quickly devised a job-sharing plan, which included allowances for time off while their children were infants. Raven stressed the productivity gains she made for her employer through this job-share initiative:

In that job share that I created, we got so much done. We got so much praise for it. It was the first job share in the company, and it was a twenty-five-year-old company. . . . I was like, "I could do this, but I only can do it half time. I can do half time, but I don't want to do it full time." . . . And I think that companies just are used to not having flexibility or offering flexibility, [and that] if they got a little bit of a nudge as an incentive, [then maybe they would do it].

Denise, too, stressed the fact that workers would be much more productive for their employers if they had flexibility. She was a thirty-year-old mother of three, ages five and under, and a MOPS member. She saw the benefits of flexibility when one of her best friends became pregnant and requested from her employer the ability to work only three days a week. The employer was receptive to the idea, and Denise witnessed firsthand how these types of arrangements can pay off.

I really think that every job opportunity, you know, every job should offer [flexibility]. If it takes the government stepping in and doing it, then so be it. . . . I think that every job should give women the opportunity to be at home, or even husbands who want to stay at home with their kids. I think they should have that opportunity, you know, as long as they're doing their job, to work it out. . . . I think that if a mom knows, "Well, okay. I have these two days off to be with my kids and do my errands that I have to do." . . . The other three days [that she's in the office], she is going to give 110 percent.

While Denise was a stay-at-home mother now, she noted that she and her husband were presently discussing if and when she should return to paid work. With a degree in education, and prior to having children, she had worked as a substitute teacher. As she pondered her options, she enthusiastically observed that securing a job in the field of education would afford her the flexibility of being home for her children when they returned from school each day. She therefore aimed to prioritize opportunities in this area when she started the nuts and bolts of the actual job hunt.

Other mothers focused on the benefit of worker retention for employers rather than productivity. Rosa, identified earlier, thirty-nine and the mother of a two-year-old girl, was a member of MomsRising.

Both she and her husband were professors. They each, therefore, had the ability to coordinate their teaching schedules around the needs of their child, who sometimes required specialized medical care. As a result of this flexibility, Rosa and her husband felt that they were consistently prepared to teach their classes, for the maximum benefit of all of their students.

> I think we have seen the impact of unfair capitalism [when there are no requirements for flexibility]. There are examples . . . that show employers really trying to do the right thing and low and behold, it costs them less to provide whatever it is that they are providing. [An example is] San Francisco and the restaurant industry. [They] have lower turnover than some of the places outside of San Francisco and it is not costing them any more even though they have paid sick leave.

Making a similar point, Anna, forty-three and the mother of five children aged five and under, was a member of NAMC. She received pay from the organization, as she was her local chapter's treasurer. This was only a part-time job, and Anna spent a significant amount of time at her children's school. While there, she noted that since many parents had to work for pay to make ends meet, they had no choice but to send their children to school even when they were very sick.

> It would be great to have people educated on how [workplace flexibility] works because if [companies] have employees who are happy and know that they can be there for their families, they're going to want to stay, they're going to work hard, and they're going to want to promote [the] business. But if . . . they need a paycheck, and they're worried about their kids at home, and oh, my God, you know, Suzy is sick, and I don't have any sick time, you know. . . . That's very scary. . . . I just think if you make your employees happy, they're going to come to work and do a good job, because they're not going to want to leave. So wouldn't you rather have people happy working for you rather than being miserable? And [what happens if they start] looking for a job and then you have to retrain other people? It doesn't make sense.

While Anna was not certain what the best form of government intervention would be, she knew that she herself was already benefitting from a flexible job, one that would be difficult to leave. She loved her job because, as she noted, she could keep up with her responsibilities as the treasurer from home if need be, including after business hours. She astutely concluded that it was the same job whether she was doing it during typical work hours or at two in the morning, and she remarked that many jobs could be made more flexible for mothers the same way.

Against a Governmental Role in Promoting Flexibility: Preference for Business Autonomy

Of course, not all mothers in the study were in favor of government intervention in the promotion of workplace flexibility. Their reasons varied, but all had a belief in business autonomy when it comes to making these employment-related decisions. On this point, some mothers argued that flexibility was important, but should be determined based on the needs of the individual firm. Wendy, thirty-seven years old and with two children, ages four and under, and a member of MomsRising, put it this way:

> There are places that are well suited to flexible schedules and flexible arrangements and there are places that just aren't. I don't have anything against giving incentives but I think incentives are better placed in other areas like giving people maternity leave. . . . But I think each business needs to decide [what to do on its own].

Wendy also maintained that since workers looked at the entire package of wages and benefits when they considered accepting a job, market forces would lead employers to offer the appropriate set of flexibility initiatives in order to compete with other firms. Others, such as NAMC member Stephanie, mentioned above, mother of two sons, one a four-year-old and the other just over one, made this point more directly, stressing that while flexibility is important, the purpose of every firm is to make money. Her views are especially noteworthy, given that earlier in this chapter she described the essential role of flexibility in making her a better parent. She had certain beliefs, however, on how flexibility should be achieved. She observed that in one of her past jobs, she worked as part of a team promoting quality assurance at a pharmaceutical company. In this group context, she formed concrete opinions about the role of government in influencing corporate human resources policy.

> My concern would be from a business standpoint; particularly a lot of the work I'm doing, [has certain requirements]. When you have so many people weighing in on one project or one document, you really do need to have sort of those core hours there that people are going to be available. You know, if people are working completely different schedules around the clock, projects like that are going to take infinitely more resources and time and money to be accomplished than they are when you know that the people you need to get a hold of are going to be at a specific place and available and working during core hours. . . . I would be concerned that it would be very challenging for the government to be able to come up with some sort of requirements that wouldn't affect that drastically and that wouldn't have a significant financial impact on businesses. . . . I think [businesses] need to have that control. I mean at the end of the day, it's a business. You know? [Businesses] are all about their revenue and their bottom line, and that's what it is.

After Stephanie had her children, she transitioned from being a full-time employee to working part time as a contract worker. She consequently lost all her benefits, but her hourly wage rate increased. In a sense, she self-engineered her own form of flexibility. Stephanie maintained that when mothers need more flexibility in their lives, they, too, should be willing to craft their own solutions rather than rely on businesses—or worse, the government—to do it for them.

Other mothers understood flexibility as potentially causing problems for employers because in many ways it is difficult to enforce employee accountability. Shannon, thirty-five and the mother of four, ages seven and under, was a member of MomsRising. She worked for her state in the field of mental health and during the course of her career had earned a master's degree. In her particular area of social work, where the health of individuals is at stake, she noted that she was constantly dealing with sensitive information that was not necessarily appropriate to computerize. Therefore, flexibility in the form of working at home on the computer was difficult for her to fully imagine. Moreover, she was concerned that there would be times when employers would not be able to adequately monitor their employees if they provided flexible work options.

> When it really comes down to it, I don't think any one rule is appropriate for anyone. What I am saying is that you should treat your employees as the adults that they are and say, "You know, as long as your work gets done, you can do this but if your work starts to slack off, then we are going to have to cut back." . . . There is an easy way to account for that. . . . You look at how things are getting done and as long as everything is operating smoothly, then what is the problem? [The problem is that] it doesn't always work that way, though.

Shannon wanted all employees to work hard and was concerned that they might not do so if some were granted greater flexibility. She also feared that resentment would build if some employees ended up feeling as if they were carrying more than their fair share of work responsibilities.

Finally, other mothers argued that it is not the responsibility of the government to get involved in workplace flexibility issues—an area where employers should be dominant—because women, as adults, are always free to "choose" their own jobs. If they want flexibility, they should simply choose a job with flexibility and not require that the government impose any type of mandate on their employer to make such offerings regular or permanent. Angela, thirty-five years old and the mother of a five-year-old girl, was a member of Mocha Moms. She explained why each woman must take responsibility for the structure of her own life, as she did when she decided to become a doctor.

> I think [flexibility] should be up to employers. I mean, ideally, when you choose a career or you accept a position, you are usually given a handbook and you know what that company expects. Now for a company, for instance, in the food service industry, if everyone took six months off, [that company] would not be able to make it. I think there are certain laws that are enacted already, you know, with the Family and Medical Leave Act that allows you to take up to twelve weeks off. . . . I think that is reasonable. I think there are things that are in place [that are working]. I don't think that the government has any business dictating what companies can and should do. I just don't think

that's something that we should get involved in and I think that as far as our freedoms, that's one of the things that makes our country special.

Interestingly, Angela was divorced, so for her economic self-sufficiency was of primary importance. However, since she had an advanced degree in medicine and was a trained chiropractor, she also had the financial resources to set her own hours by having her own practice. She believed that just as she had been able to advance her education and achieve her dreams in this way, so should all mothers across the United States.

Mixed Reactions to a Governmental Role in Promoting Flexibility

Of course, not every mother's reaction was black and white when it came to the government's role in promoting workplace flexibility. Numerous mothers had mixed feelings about the idea of government intervention in labor market arrangements. Sherry, thirty-eight years old and a MomsRising member, was one of these mothers. She argued that businesses need fewer regulations in order to operate successfully in the free market, especially in difficult economic downturns. With three children under the age of twelve at home, however, she also understood the pressures families are under and how they could benefit from any policies designed to help them more adequately integrate their work and family lives.

> I hate to say it but especially in this economic climate, you really have to make [workplace flexibility] feasible for the businesses. You can't mandate it or it is just not going to work. . . . [But at the same time] the health of the worker and the family members is paramount and if you have sick families or tired-out families, you are just going to suffer at work. I don't think everybody knows that but especially in today's society, people are pushed, especially with technology making everything so instant. You are pushed to do more and more and more and have a higher job performance for less pay. . . . We know that employers would benefit if the workers were healthier and happier. . . . I think that with the structure of having to have dual-income families, you have to have [flexibility]. Something has to give.

Sherry was able to see the issue from the perspective of both the employer and the employee. Partly this resulted from her own personal experiences in each role. On the one hand, she noted that earlier in her career, she had worked in an engineering and architectural firm for eight years. She had been assigned to a team and had to work collaboratively with others. She reported understanding why her company did not offer flexibility: team personnel had to be there during core business hours to respond to client needs. On the other hand, as the business environment became more difficult with the recession, she was laid off and became a part-time interior design teacher. Her supervisor allowed her to choose her own classes and set her own hours. This experience revealed to her the benefits of flexibility, especially when her children were young. At the time of her interview, then, her opinions on workplace flexibility overall were fluid.

Other mothers also had mixed feelings about the government's role in flexibility, but these were mostly about the *nature* of that role rather than merely the presence or absence of the role itself. Heather, a forty-one-year-old NAMC member and the mother of a six-year-old boy and a five-year-old girl, argued against government mandates as they related to flexibility, but she was open to government-sponsored educational efforts and tax incentives.

> While I may disagree with making laws or having requirements, I think the government definitely has a role in promoting and kind of calling out good examples and certainly trying to find ways that would help facilitate flexible work arrangements [for workers].

In addition to identifying the type of governmental role she would support, Heather emphasized that it would have to make sense for companies in this profit-driven world to offer flexibility. For example, she was currently an outreach director for a nonprofit organization that promoted the use of open-source software. While on occasion she had to travel for her job, most of the time she worked from her own home computer and could set her own hours. She noted that while she benefited from this flexibility, it was because her job just happened to be structured in this fashion. For other jobs, such a flexible arrangement might not be possible, and decisions on such matters should be left to employers.

Finally, other mothers supported flexibility to a certain extent but argued that small businesses should be exempt. Irene, thirty-five, a MOPS member and the mother of two girls under the age seven, discussed the pros and cons of flexibility as she saw them from her personal family background.

> I struggle with this. This is a very Republican-versus-Democrat kind of question. My dad owns his own small business and he has been in business for twenty years, so I see him operate. For the government to come in and say, "Well, this business has ten employees, [so] you have to follow these procedures and hire this percentage of working mothers, blah, blah, blah"—that would be devastating to him. . . . Maybe it makes sense that for small businesses, you get some tax breaks or credits that would make it easier for you to do it, and then if you are a bigger business, you start getting into punitive measures. . . . Some of the bigger firms should be pulling more of their own weight in my opinion. . . . In many ways, it is good business. . . . Employers need to be more flexible.

Irene noted wistfully that prior to having her first baby, she worked as a human resources manager up to fifty-five hours a week, which included extensive travel. At that time, her company had only about sixty employees and therefore it was not feasible for her supervisors to offer flexibility options. After her maternity leave, Irene was offered her old job back, but because of her responsibilities caring for her child, she declined to accept it. Over the past several years, the firm had grown tremendously and now had over six hundred employees. As she understood it, along with this growth, the company had become much more family friendly regarding workplace flexibility initiatives. Irene believed that this change was appropriate, especially given the firm's new size, and hoped that mothers in the firm would appreciate these new options now at their fingertips.

Undoubtedly, modern mothers are feeling the squeeze. They experience role conflict when work and family demands occur at the same time and they cannot possibly satisfy both sets of tasks simultaneously. They drown in role overload when the cumulative pressures of both work and family become insurmountable. But there is a way out. Workplace flexibility policy options offer mothers opportunities to engage in rewarding work and family experiences by giving them more control over their work schedule. Indeed, for significant percentages of group members and for both mothers who currently work for pay and mothers who stay at home, certain types of flexibility policies were rated as critical as they imagined their ideal jobs. Flexible start and stop times, compressed workweeks, advance knowledge about overtime and shift schedules, part-time work, short-term time off, regular time off, and extended time off were very important across the board—for all sets of mothers. In the interviews, mothers also revealed *why* they prized flexibility. Stay-at-home mothers valued flexibility that would enable them to provide their children with maximum direct care around their employment schedules, help them pursue promising employment opportunities, and control who would be involved in taking care of their children when they are not available. Mothers who currently work for pay valued flexibility but for different reasons. They argued that such policies would enable them to be better parents, be more energized employees, and feel more respected by their employers.

Given this noteworthy overlap in preferences among mothers, is there any consensus about what to do about it? The simple answer is yes. The majority of mothers agreed that the government has a strong role in educating businesses, as well as providing them with awards, grants, and incentives to help promote flexibility. Only requirements on businesses, especially mandated flexibility offerings, received significantly less support from mothers in all groups, and regardless of current paid work status. In the interviews, mothers who agreed with some role for government involvement maintained that there is a unique place for intervention in this area of the economy and that the private sector would not do much on its own. A smaller number who disagreed with government intervention stated that businesses should have maximum autonomy in determining their employment practices, or that, in crafting public policy, business interests should at least be considered. A final set of mothers stressed the needs of both employers and employees when these mothers made the case for a more moderate role for government in advancing workplace flexibility.

Overall, however, the take-away message from this chapter is that there is strong convergence among the majority of mothers about what they want in terms of workplace flexibility, and how to get there. The next critical question then becomes, Do they have the will to form a political movement to make it happen?

6

Are We in a Movement Now?
Can We Get There?

*As an online community, MomsRising members typically do not en-
counter each other face to face, but that does not hold them back when
it comes to expressing themselves during an online chat designed to
elicit their opinions on important topical issues of motherhood. Various people move in and out of the hour-long afternoon chat that takes
place on a crisp fall day. At one point, the conversation becomes especially animated when these mothers are asked whether they believe
they are part of a mothers' movement and what issues they would like
to see such a movement stress.*

MomsRising Member 1: Yes! We are amid a mothers' movement!

MomsRising Member 2: Yes. This is a mothers' movement.

MomsRising Member 3: As a nonmother . . . I think of myself as supporting the mothers' movement.

MomsRising Member 4: I think of this as an offshoot of the women's
movement. The work of second- and third-wave feminists hasn't
been successfully accomplished until these issues we're talking
about are part of the fabric of our daily work lives.

MomsRising Member 5: I see it as an evolution of the same women's
movement starting way back to Elizabeth Cady Stanton, etc. [It is
not] separate.

MOMSRISING MEMBER 6: Yes, [I think it is a mothers' movement]. In May 2007, the Equal Employment Opportunity Commission even came out with guidelines. [These guidelines explain how certain treatment against workers with caregiving responsibilities might constitute discrimination based on sex, disability, or other characteristics that are granted protection by federal employment discrimination laws.]

MOMSRISING MEMBER 7: We need family-friendly policies so our country can move forward. [However,] I do not think enough people see [these issues] as important.

MOMSRISING MEMBER 2: The people at Mothers & More call it "the unfinished work of the feminist movement."

MOMSRISING MEMBER 1: I think we can put political views aside and join in agreement [with other mothers' groups] on legislating work-life benefits.

MOMSRISING MEMBER 6: I agree that [the mothers' movement] is part of the women's movement—but maybe we are closer to a revolution!

MOMSRISING MEMBER 2: We'll work together when we can with [other mothers' groups]. . . . Harmony is overrated.

MOMSRISING MEMBER 5: I think the sentiment earlier, "we all make our choices for our reasons," is vital to keep in mind when interfacing with other mothers' groups.

MOMSRISING MEMBER 8: Yes, I do believe [that] the last generation of women paved the way through the corporate/law school/medical school/etc. doors and our generation will pave the way for our daughters to be unapologetic moms who are also professionals.

MOMSRISING MEMBER 4: It is [a movement]. Totally!! The feminist movement is the movement of all women, with and without children, and I think that it is the hardest for moms, with all they have to deal with, to be an active part [of this and to carve out their own piece of this].

MOMSRISING MEMBER 1: The mothers' movement should stress flextime and telecommuting in the workplace, along with fair pay and affordable child care.

The clear majority of this set of MomsRising members, as demonstrated in the online discussion excerpted above, clearly believed that they are participating in a new type of mothers' movement, or a social movement based on their identities as mothers. In this online exchange, members not only expressed support for the idea that they are part of a mothers' movement but also honed in on how their mothers' movement differed from political campaigns of the past, which focused on such issues as health, education, reproduction, financial well-being, breastfeeding, substance abuse, and gun violence, as described in chapter 1. Instead, these modern mothers discussed the issue they seemed to think would most likely draw women together: workplace flexibility. But interestingly, they noted that not all mothers would share their view of mobilization, or in one member's perspective: "We'll work together when we can. . . . Harmony is overrated."

It has been demonstrated in this book that among mothers' group members, there is a strong interest in the topic of workplace flexibility and that it generates significant support. All organizations in this study have public positions on a variety of workplace flexibility issues; some of their goals are based on individual responsibility and well-being and others on active policy change at the macro level. But do most women look beyond their own individual group affiliation to think about mothers acting together on behalf of workplace flexibility? Or are they not inclined toward collective action, either now or in the future?

Creating a widespread and sustainable mothers' movement is a central mission of those who wish to promote workplace flexibility as a national issue, yet the road by which a mother may come to link herself with a larger mothers' movement is extremely complex.[1] That is, individuals are quite variable in both their likelihood of taking part in any type of political activity and in the intensity of their efforts if and when they do decide to engage.[2] Individuals choosing to identify themselves with a *specific* social movement are similarly variable. Often what is significant in this decision and commitment process is the establishment of a common collective identity—composed of a prospective movement's boundaries, goals, and vision—that speaks to people's needs and desires for richer lives.[3] This collective identity can be likened to a movement's culture, which serves to energize members, encourage dedication to the cause, and present options for reform to those with the power to overhaul policy in the public arena.[4] Understanding the strength of this collective identity, or the culture of an emerging mothers' movement, is therefore critical to mapping out its potential for future impact.

Are They in a Mothers' Movement Right Now?

As demonstrated at the beginning of this book, women join mothers' organizations for diverse reasons, among them emotional support and adult friendship, friendship for their children, information about parenting resources and techniques, and opportunities for engagement in public policy and political activism. While some of these reasons might lead them to think about their involvement rather narrowly and at the community level only, other considerations may help them conceptualize their participation much more broadly, as part of a mothers' movement. But initial inducements to join are only one part of the picture. Groups can shape individuals' attitudes *after* they join, encouraging members to think about issues in new ways and to identify with the collective identity of the larger political movement.[5] In this way, individuals come to be attracted to what they perceive as the collective identity of their group, and groups like them, and are willing to work on their behalf. This broader level of identification, however, has not happened yet among the majority of mothers' group members studied here. On average, according to the survey data in table 6.1, only 36.4 percent of all group mothers currently believe they are part of a mothers' movement, with a range from 22.8 percent for MOPS members to 65.7 percent for MomsRising members. In terms of the breakdown by employment status, numbers are slightly higher for mothers working for pay (40.4%) than for mothers staying at home (32.3%).

In the interview data, the 125 respondents were approximately evenly divided when questioned about whether they thought of themselves as currently being part of a mothers' movement, with sixty-four saying no, fifty-six saying yes, and five being unsure. They explained their responses by primarily focusing on their view of the group's role in their daily lives and in the modern social world (table 6.2).

TABLE 6.1.
Do you believe that you are participating in a mothers' movement right now? (%)

	All group mothers	All employed group mothers	All stay-at-home group mothers	NAMC	MomsRising	MOPS	Mocha Moms	Mothers & More
Yes	36.4	40.4	32.3	36.8	65.7	22.8	45.4	29.8
No	63.6	59.6	67.7	63.2	34.3	77.2	54.6	70.2

TABLE 6.2.
Participating in a mothers' movement right now? Themes from the interviews (%)

	All group mothers	NAMC	Moms Rising	MOPS	Mocha Moms	Mothers & More
Movement deniers: groups are there to help them with the challenges of everyday life	48.8	60	32	52	60	40
Movement affirmers: groups are redefining motherhood	13.6	4	12	24	0	28
Movement affirmers: groups are solving common motherhood problems	12.8	8	12	16	4	24
Movement affirmers: groups are focused on mothers' issues across the country	10.4	32	0	0	20	0

Movement Deniers: Our Groups Focus on the Challenges We Face as Mothers in Our Daily Lives

For mothers who answered that they did not believe that they are participating in a mothers' movement right now, almost all gave the same reason. Their involvement was simply not directed toward a broader goal of mass organization for political purposes. Instead, they viewed their attachment to their groups as much more focused on helping them with the everyday challenges of fulfilling their family roles. For some, this perspective was based on their preferred type of involvement with their group, and for others, it had more to do with the opportunities the group offered them.

Judith, described earlier, twenty-five and the mother of two boys aged three years and six months, was a member of MOPS. She was adamant in her denial of being part of a mothers' movement, with her opinion growing from her current load of parenting responsibilities and the division of labor in her household. Her husband was an attorney who worked long hours, and while her degree was in the education field, recall that she worked at her local hospital's emergency room intake center on an on-call basis during the weekends. This schedule enabled her to attend to the majority of her children's needs, but she still frequently felt overwhelmed by her caretaking responsibilities.

> I am far too busy to put that kind of effort into anything. I have mothers [in my group] who have children and are going through the same thing. We connect on many levels because we very much understand what each other is going through. I have a very busy, active life because I am chasing after two little children all day long and it's all I can do to check e-mail or get a phone call.

In a similar way, Victoria, thirty-five, a MomsRising member and the mother of a four-year-old son, stated that she simply did not have the time to invest more of her energies into a broader, social movement.

> I don't [think I am part of a larger movement] because it always seems that I am always involved in the day-to-day things that my son and I are going through. . . . I just don't know if I have the time to [be involved].

Victoria was extremely busy. She worked full time at a cancer research center without any flexibility. She had never married her child's father, and he was completely uninvolved in their lives. This left her without any type of child care coverage during the week and for emergencies. Interestingly, however, in her interview, Victoria did state that while she currently did not believe she was part of a mothers' movement, she wished that she did have the time to become more attentive to broader social change campaigns that could improve mothers' lives in the future. The daily tasks associated with taking care of her son, however, prevented her from taking any type of action right now.

While these mothers were simply too busy to consider any larger purposes related to a mothers' movement regardless of what goals their groups put forward, other mothers deliberately sought out groups that they thought would focus on only narrow community-based and family-life issues. Irene, identified earlier, thirty-five and a MOPS member, was the mother of two girls, ages six and three.

I do not consider [my group as being part of] a movement. I just consider it a matter of survival. If I were going to be a mom, I just need to be the best that I could be and if there were a tool that would help me do it, [I wanted to find it]. I did not join MOPS thinking, "Gosh, I am going to change the world." It is just a matter of . . . "I need to improve my [mothering] skills." . . . I do not see what MOPS is doing as revolutionary. I do not see it as anything new. It is probably more formal and more structured but it is [helping with] stuff that has been going on since the beginning of time.

In Irene's view, MOPS-sponsored activities replaced extended family-generated activities that used to emerge more organically within communities. Since many parents now feared allowing their children any type of socially interactive freedom with people who just happened to live on their streets, they used MOPS as a new, substitute network with which to establish trustworthy ties.

In each of the preceding cases, mothers' preferences defined how they viewed their group participation as limited in scope and not as part of a broader mothers' movement. Other mothers, however, stated that much to their chagrin, their groups themselves were not currently set up to pursue broader goals. Diane, thirty-seven, was a NAMC member. She had two girls, ages five and two, and was somewhat frustrated with the direction in which her group had been going recently.

I wish I could answer that [my group] was [part of] something that's like a real movement, you know, [and] that we're really politically active. I know that there are such movements afoot, and I want to pay more attention to them and be involved with them. Honestly, as it exists now, [our group] is more of a local support group—you know, [providing] socialization activities for our kids.

In a similar way, thirty-four-year-old Tina, referred to earlier, admitted that her group had not taken on a broader perspective that might be appropriate for a mothers' movement. Recall that she had a two-year-old daughter and a five-month-old son and was a member of Mothers & More. Although the national organization had a clear, wide-ranging agenda to improve the lives of mothers everywhere, Tina did not experience that emphasis in her local chapter.

I have not really been engaged on a political level as part of a "mothers' movement" right now, but it might be something? Just having this conversation has sort of sparked [in me that], okay, maybe that would be an interesting thing to focus on. I definitely know that there are a few groups out there that are focusing on much greater efforts and such and that would be really interesting. As of right now, [however], no, I do not feel that I am part of a movement per se.

Both Diane and Tina described a phenomenon that is common to many of these groups. Although they all promote specific fellowship and policy goals on their national websites, whether these goals are actually implemented depends on the priorities of the local chapter. For a social movement perspective to emerge, mothers need to see how its objectives fit into their busy daily lives in a meaningful way, and some local chapters are not making a concerted effort to fulfill this purpose.

In contrast with the mothers who denied that they were part of a mothers' movement because either they did not seek out this larger goal or their group did not offer them this possibility, mothers who stated that they were part of a movement cited three distinct reasons. They believed that they are part of a mothers' movement because their affiliation is (1) helping them redefine the meaning of motherhood, (2) assisting them in educating others about solving common problems of motherhood, and (3) aiding them in spreading the word about mothers' issues across the country.

Movement Affirmers: Groups Are Redefining the Meaning of Motherhood

For some mothers, redefining motherhood on their own terms was central to their belief that they belong to a mothers' movement; this was the first most commonly reported theme on this point. These mothers had frequently experienced different patterns of work and staying at home and viewed being part of a mothers' movement as a way to remove the stigma from each of these arrangements. As Josephine, a thirty-seven-year-old MomsRising member and the mother of three

daughters, a three-year-old and five-year-old twins, put it, in a mothers'
movement, mothers have the power to redefine the popular imagery associated with their work-life arrangements.

> Mothers are changing so much these days, from the stay-at-home
> [mothers] in the sixties to the power women of the nineties. Yes, [we
> can try to] just be part of [supporting those changes]. I am a stay-at-
> home mom but I am still a part of this society. . . . We have been out
> there. We've done what we thought we wanted to do but now we want
> to stay home. We want to be with our kids. This is what we want. We
> are choosing this. We are not being forced into this. It's something
> we want. It's not because in our minds, society is telling us that is
> what we are supposed to do. We've kind of gone out and experienced
> life and we will [stay at home or work for pay] and maybe we will do
> something else later. . . . So I see that and I am hoping more and more
> people will start to see that, too.

Other mothers, like Josephine, insisted that they are part of a mothers' movement because of the important work that needs to be done in
altering negative judgments associated with different arrangements in
mothers' work-family lives. Julia was one such mother, who, at thirty-
five, was a Mothers & More member and had two boys, ages three years
and eight months.

> I would like to think [that I am in a movement]. . . . My generation of
> mothers were trying to forge a middle ground. [We had to work out]
> the whole, Do you work part-time, do you work full-time, or do you
> stay at home? This idea that there is a middle or that it is okay to
> move in and out [was novel but we were pushing for it]. We are try-
> ing to remind everybody that we are still respectable people. We are
> still really trying to make that more mainstream. . . . [We are sort of
> saying], Hey, everybody else, stop pigeonholing us and stop telling us
> that we have to be one or the other or else there is something wrong
> with us.

Both Josephine and Julia felt strongly that previous generations of mothers had worked hard to widen the scope of opportunities available to
them, especially in the paid labor market. Identifying with the current

mothers' movement, they hoped to make an even wider range of arrangements in paid employment acceptable to society at large.

Josephine and Julia remained committed to changing society's attitudes toward motherhood through their identification with a mothers' movement. Other mothers were more focused on the ways in which a movement could redefine motherhood by bringing mothers with different arrangements of paid work together rather than keeping them apart. Selena, mentioned earlier, thirty-eight and a Mothers & More member with three children aged six and under, stated:

> Yes, I guess I do consider myself part of a mothers' movement by being part of Mothers & More and being aware of the major issues that face mothers. . . . I think it is just important for mothers to be supportive of other mothers because sometimes it is very easy to feel isolated and alone. . . . That is the case when you are alone with young children. . . . Many working mothers are working in environments where there are not always other working mothers, and their peers do not always get where they are at, or where they are coming from, or all the hardships they went through just to get out the door in the morning. It is really important for mothers to recognize and support each other, for the value of their role in society, whether they are working or staying at home. . . . [It is important] to not build dividers based on [one's paid work status] but just to try to be supportive and friendly toward each other. Like school things, maybe the stay-at-home mom can pick up one of the working mom's kids and bring [the child] home after school, eat out or something, so the working mom can do something else or the stay-at-home mom can [do something else for the working mom]. [The point is] not to divide but to try to build connectivity among all mothers with whom you come in contact in your everyday life, and to try to build those relationships. You do not have to be best friends, but just provide some friendly smiles to be supportive of each other during a busy time in everyone's life.

Judy, identified earlier, thirty-seven and a MOPS member, reflected Selena's sentiments in identifying with a mothers' movement that brings women together rather than divides them. With a five-year-old daughter and a three-year-old son at home, Judy recognized the importance of this support between mothers.

> I think it is good to have a connection [with mothers of different back-grounds]. I think it is good to be able to find differences in other family types, whether extended or blended and those types of things. . . . I hope that moms' groups will grow. MOPS is not to just be there for mothers who stay at home. We are also here for mothers who work, who struggle between finding a balance between working, being a mother, and being a wife and finding time for all of those [roles]. We are open to all of it. We are not discriminatory toward that.

In her interview, Judy expressed a desire for MOPS to continue to grow and have a positive impact on women's lives. The group's Christian orientation was one of its key strengths because it helped put the focus on the importance of the family as *an entire unit* in raising children, and in this it included a key role for fathers. Interestingly, Judy stressed that flexibility should be a rallying cry for all mothers, promoting flexibility not only for themselves but also for their partners. In this new workplace model, fathers must be key players as caregivers for their children, and flexibility would afford them enhanced opportunities to play this role.

Movement Affirmers: Groups Are Educating Women to Solve Common Motherhood Problems

The second most common theme that emerged from mothers who believed that they are part of a mothers' movement was their feeling that they are engaged in a larger intellectual project to solve common problems of motherhood. Barbara, sixty, had two adult daughters and was still involved in NAMC. In her interview, Barbara described how she helped women view their personal struggles with combining work and family as a potentially wider-ranging political struggle for mothers' rights.

> I feel [like] I'm part of a mothers' movement partly because one of our founders has been talking about a mothers' movement for thirty years. So we were talking in that way, way before the current crop of mothers' groups and mothers' pundits started talking about it. So we always, organizationally, saw the empowerment of women, informed

choice, as very crucial to society. . . . And I feel like I'm part of that because I lead an organization that helps to raise the consciousness of women. [It] helps to train them in critical thinking, in making informed choices, and in asking for the information that they need without just going along with something because someone tells them that they should be doing it. [It] helps them advocate for themselves, their children, and their families in every aspect of their lives. And [it] helps them identify the common issues that they think, when they first get to us, are really personal issues. [Sometimes they come in thinking,] "I decided to have a job so now I have to live with the consequences." And we're saying, "But what are your choices around that and are they good enough?" And [let's think about] comparing what do we do here with what other countries are doing. . . . So I feel that we are definitely participating in a mothers' movement, because we're on the side of educating the women about the issues and encouraging them personally to get involved. And [we encourage them] that they can make a difference, even if for just for one person. . . . And, you know, if you get involved in the political process, you can make a difference for a larger number of people, but even what you might do in your own Mothers' Center, even what you might do when you are home with a newborn and feeling overwhelmed, your sharing of your birth story with another mother is an act of advocacy.

In many ways, Barbara echoed the views of women involved in the feminist movement of the 1960s and 1970s, when "the personal is political" became a rallying cry to encourage a higher level of consciousness among women about their common plight. Joan in many ways expanded on the mechanisms that Barbara had articulated about how she believed mothers could foment change, simply by giving voice to their common problems. Identified earlier, Joan was a thirty-year-old MOPS member and the mother of five girls aged seven and under. She emphasized how she came to participate in what she viewed as a larger social movement. This involved pointing out to others how previously conceptualized personal issues and problems can be thought of more broadly—as issues affecting mothers nationwide.

I think people are paying a lot of attention to moms for different reasons. [They're paying attention] not just to the candy, flowers, and dinner at Mother's Day, but to the everyday issues that moms deal with that we are vocal about with one another. [In the past], mothers have not felt comfortable enough to be vocal about [these issues] in mainstream [life]. . . . People just did not hear it because we complain about it to ourselves or we have that guilt that [other mothers are] taking care of everything. [We worried to ourselves if we could not] even get our three-year-old potty trained or our four-year-old off a pacifier. [But there are changes now]. It is not a huge, big deal [right now], but there are marches and there are quiet little battles being won locally [in terms of promoting] the mothers' movement.

Joan, like many other women in the study, viewed herself as highly political. She voted in every election, including local ones, and was considering running for her town's school board at the time of her interview. Mothers like Joan hoped that by raising awareness about common problems at the grassroots level, they would help start a contagion of political activity on mothers' issues across the country.

Another set of mothers perceived that they were part of a mothers' movement less through examining the actions of the previous women's movement than in their directly educating other women about better possible options for work and family life. Recall that Louise, thirty-six, had a three-year-old son and was a member of Mothers & More. As a stay-at-home mother, she asserted that her identification with the mothers' movement predominantly came through informing others about new ways to think about their caretaking responsibilities.

I think that a lot of times stay-at-home moms associate that [label] with being the typical 1950s mom. You cook, you clean, and you do all the kids' stuff, all of the child care. [However, the new feeling that we are promoting is that] yes, sure, I am a stay-at-home parent, but it does not mean that I have to be that stereotypical type of mother. . . . I think it is important to know that just because I stay at home now does not mean that I do not want to work. Ideally, I think any woman would like to be able to stay home and be paid to take care of her kids. . . . In other countries, folks get stipends for being at home with their kids versus working or getting paid leave for leaving their job and raising their children. . . . There [are options] for that.

While Louise was not optimistic that such changes would come readily to the United States without significant advocacy efforts, the existence of alternative paradigms in other countries gave her something to point to when mothers questioned the restrictive confines of their own lives. While Louise looked toward government policies in other nations to promote more expansive opportunities for mothers in the United States, Jane, described earlier, a thirty-seven-year-old MOPS member and mother of two, pointed to what she viewed as the liberation of the Bible in educating women about their options.

> As I mentioned to you before, the women who are my contemporaries are choosing to stay home. Ironically, many of our mothers chose to work. That being said, I think a lot of us . . . are finding a way to use our creativity to say, yes, you are at home, but that does not mean you are at home 24/7 throughout the calendar year. We are plotting a [new] course. We are finding a niche where [society] says you cannot have it all, but we are accomplishing that. We are doing for our children, we are doing for our families and that is where our first priority is; however, we are doing something else over here. We explore ourselves and there is a very biblical example for that. . . . Have you ever heard of the Proverbs 31 woman? The thirty-first chapter of Proverbs describes, from a biblical standpoint, the ideal woman and it goes through the whole list of all these things that she does for her family. Then one of the verses says she considers a vineyard, buys it, and makes a profit. So . . . she works at home, she takes care of her children, and she takes care of her family, but on the side, she is looking out for some type of business venture. That is when I think that women of faith, particularly, are excelling. They are being creative, they are taking care of their family—that is their number one priority—but they are looking outside the box for something of their own.

Importantly, Jane noted that mothers do not need to search for external professional outlets when their children are young; she believed that small children need their mothers on a full-time basis. However, Jane interpreted the Bible as encouraging mothers to pursue other interests, including those involving business, once their children reach a certain, more mature age. It was simply up to mothers' groups, in Jane's view, to educate women on this important new fulfilling direction for their lives.

Movement Affirmers: Groups Are Spreading the Word on Mothers' Issues across the Country

Finally, and the third most commonly reported theme here, mothers identified with the mothers' movement because they could observe activities and progress on behalf of issues critical to them beyond their local group. For some mothers, this meant witnessing interactions in their local chapters and in the national organization to promote positive change for mothers. Angela, referred to earlier, thirty-five and a member of Mocha Moms with one daughter aged five, argued that she had a strong mothers' movement identification because of the unity with which the national group worked with the local chapters in identifying common needs and satisfying them.

> Mocha Moms as a whole does a lot for the community and since we are all over the United States, there are various chapters. Even though [you know] locally we make an impact, but nationally [when] you look at the number of members that we have, [they are enormous]. . . . I mean, we have national conferences and things like that as well [to unify the organization]. . . . [This helps get us] all on the same page, so it's not something that's just [taking place] locally.

While Angela focused on the interaction between the local groups and the national office to demonstrate that she is part of a movement, Briana, thirty-five and the mother of four children aged seven and under, considered herself part of a mothers' movement through her affiliation with Mocha Moms because of the ways in which the national organization personally involved her in important motherhood issues. Her heightened awareness of mothers' issues was not spontaneous, but emerged gradually as she became more attuned to what the national group was doing.

> If you would have asked me that question initially, meaning a couple of years ago, I would have said it was just local support for me and the people around [me]. But with the e-mails that I keep getting [from the national office, I started feeling more involved]. . . . So it seems more [like a movement] with all the e-mails and all that, and, you

know, [the national group is trying to get] Michelle Obama to go to the national convention. . . . You know, there's a letter-writing campaign for that, so the more that I'm starting to read into that, the more [I feel] like I am part of a movement. . . . It's [about] trying to juggle it all, working and having kids, and having the best, well-rounded children that you can. Of course, it's all motherhood issues.

For yet other mothers, it was their interaction with mothers from other group chapters across the country that gave them a more national perspective and led them to identify with a mothers' movement. Heather, mentioned earlier, forty-one, first joined her local NAMC group with specific goals to help her raise her six-year-old son and five-year-old daughter. She wanted to get out of the house and be with other mothers who understood the developmental issues that she was facing with her children at the time. She later became a leader of her local group. In this position of authority, she was able to communicate regularly with other NAMC chapter leaders. This communication enabled her to process two kinds of information that fundamentally transformed her into an engaged, politicized individual:

> I was involved as a leader in my group. I got to know the leaders of NAMC and spent a lot of time kind of talking about the micro issues, which I would call kind of interpersonal issues relative to my mothers' group. But I also got to learn about the macro issues relative to the community at large and the United States at large, including the more social issues like the Mommy Wars and stuff like that.

From the foundation point as her group leader, then, Heather was able to expand her notion of mothers' issues beyond those that concerned her local circle of friends. Once she assumed this new position, she decided to reorient the focus of her group, going beyond organizing activities and offering information for mothers in her town, to promoting discussion "circles" around important work-family issues. These newly implemented discussion circles included both online forums and regularly scheduled conversations in person about the pressures of being "superwoman" in modern society and how best to conquer everyday stressors and optimize one's time.

Should Mothers Form a Mothers' Movement, and What Should the Issues Be?

Although the majority of mothers in the survey and interviews did not believe that they were in a mothers' movement right now, as noted above, those who did have such beliefs were passionate about them. More compellingly, a significant majority of both those surveyed and those interviewed argued that mothers should form such a movement in the future. Indeed, as table 6.3 shows, 63.5 percent of all group mothers agreed with such an action, ranging from 38.6 percent of MOPS members to 89 percent of MomsRising members. In addition, this number reached 70 percent among all mothers currently working for pay and was still over half for stay-at-home mothers, at 56.7 percent. When those who agreed that mothers should form a movement were asked on what issues this mobilization should focus, workplace flexibility dominated other policy concerns such as health care, education, after-school programs, child care, and pay equity for mothers, at 42.7 percent (table 6.4). On the individual group level, these numbers ranged from 35 percent of MomsRising members to 49 percent of Mothers & More members. Interestingly, the percentage of stay-at-home mothers rating workplace flexibility as the most important issue was higher than that of mothers working for pay (46.9% vs. 39.4%). Overall, these data show that overwhelmingly, although MOPS members lagged slightly behind, most mothers believed that a movement would be helpful to them, regardless of their current paid employment status, and that workplace flexibility should be a top policy priority of this mobilization.

The mothers in the interviews were asked to react to slightly different questions about their future as a collective unit. Instead of responding to whether they believed mothers should form a movement in the upcoming years, the respondents were asked to assume that a mothers' movement would definitely emerge in the near future. Given this prediction, did they believe workplace flexibility would be an important issue around which all mothers could rally? The brief answer was yes. Mothers, in fact, were overwhelmingly optimistic about this possibility. In fact, when queried about this issue directly, ninety-one agreed that it was a strong enough issue to create a movement, thirty-nine disagreed, and five were unsure. Overall, then, while a minority of women believed that workplace flexibility was not a significant enough

TABLE 6.3.
Should mothers come together in a social movement? (%)

	All group mothers	All employed group mothers	All stay-at-home group mothers	NAMC	MomsRising	MOPS	Mocha Moms	Mothers & More
Yes	63.5	70	56.7	74.6	89	38.6	75.9	61.4
No	36.0	30	43.3	25.4	11	61.4	24.1	38.6

TABLE 6.4.
What is the most important issue this mothers' movement should focus on? (%)

	All group mothers	All employed group mothers	All stay-at-home group mothers	NAMC	MomsRising	MOPS	Mocha Moms	Mothers & More
Workplace flexibility for mothers	42.7	39.4	46.9	44.7	35.0	38.2	40.6	49.0
Health care for children	15.1	17.2	12.5	11.7	20.3	14.8	13.5	14.2
Education	18.5	15.9	22	15.9	12.3	30.0	24.8	14.3
Afterschool programs	0.3	0.3	0.2	0.8	0.5	0	0.4	10.0
Child care	12.8	16.7	7.7	15.2	14.5	10.2	11.2	13.3
Pay equity for mothers	10.8	10.5	10.7	12.2	17.5	6.7	9.8	9.0

TABLE 6.5.
Can workplace flexibility be a rallying point for a mothers' movement? (%)

	All group mothers	NAMC	Moms Rising	MOPS	Mocha Moms	Mothers & More
Yes, workplace flexibility can benefit all mothers	23.2	48	12	16	16	24
Yes, workplace flexibility can help mothers best manage their lives	11.2	4	16	4	24	8
No, workplace flexibility not strong enough to build a movement	13.6	12	12	24	8	12

issue around which to mobilize or would require too much consensus building to become important among all mothers, the great majority of mothers in this study asserted that workplace flexibility was a straightforward issue around which to unite women into a solid social movement. They offered multiple reasons for this viewpoint, including that it has the potential to benefit all mothers in making paid work decisions—even those currently at home—and that mothers need flexibility to best manage their lives (table 6.5)

Workplace Flexibility as Benefiting All Mothers in Making Paid Work Decisions

The first and most commonly cited theme among mothers regarding why workplace flexibility could be a galvanizing issue for a mothers' movement was their belief in its potential to bring all women together, whether currently working for pay or staying at home. This was because it widened the scope of options to women as they considered the paid work decision. Virginia, a thirty-four-year-old NAMC member and mother of three children aged six and under, described her view of how mothers working for pay and staying at home would see the common importance of this issue.

I think that everybody, regardless of whether they work or not, can appreciate the benefits of [workplace flexibility]. I think a lot of even stay-at-home moms envision going back to work at some point. They may not be interested in going back full time when . . . their kids are in school, [but even then] it's nice still to work part time. You can work while they're at school and be home when they're at home. . . . But I think it's just something that benefits everybody, and even if it's not for you, it could be for your husband. You know? Having that flexibility [is key].

Karen, twenty-eight years old with twin five-year-old daughters and a member of Mocha Moms, agreed with Virginia's assessment.

Well, I think, actually both [working for pay and stay-at-home mothers would benefit from workplace flexibility policies]. Well, of course, [these policies would help] moms who work for pay . . . because they would make their lives easier. But even stay-at-home moms [would benefit]. . . . If they felt like they were able to get into a work environment, or work for an employer who would allow them to make their own hours or do . . . job sharing and stuff, where they're still able to be available for their families when they need to be, I think more of them would be more inclined to work. [They could also] fulfill some of their goals and aspirations while they have small children or children who are in middle school. . . . So I think that there would be a consensus there.

For Karen, workplace flexibility gives mothers the opportunity to fulfill different dreams that they might have beyond taking care of their children. Amanda viewed workplace flexibility the same way, as opening the doors to new options that mothers might not yet know they have available to them. With five-year-old twin girls at home, Amanda, thirty-six, was a member of NAMC.

I think that [workplace flexibility] would open your choices, and if you knew [you had these policies in place, you might do things differently]. So many people I know are not even considering going back to work until their children are older, because . . . flextime work in a professional environment is very hard to find. I think that people might make different choices, or at least feel that they . . . had more options, let's say, if there were a bigger push toward flexible work arrangements.

Prior to the birth of her children, Amanda worked in the field of human resources. She had a full-time job and worked very long hours. Her daughters were born premature and needed a lot of attention; therefore, her original plan of returning to her job part time never materialized. She needed to be at home, and fortunately, her husband earned enough to support the family. Other mothers, Amanda recognized, were clearly in her position in having had a quality job but then having to confront life events that could be managed only by having additional time-off options. Flexibility would offer them these types of choices, especially if they could not financially afford to return home completely.

Dorothy, a Mocha Moms member, echoed the views of many mothers in the study when she described the commonalities that bound them all together and should make workplace flexibility a very important public policy goal to achieve.

> Our priority is our children. . . . So, being a stay-at-home mom, the priority is the children, and being a working mom, the priority is the children. So, in other words, [right] now, I am a stay-at-home mom, [but] I do plan on reentering the workforce. . . . I have one going to school and the other one [is ready] to go. But I do plan on going back [to work], and therefore, the flextime [is key to me]. . . . It does not matter if you are a stay-at-home mom or a working mom, we all agree that our priority is our children, so the flextime will give us [the time we need with them].

At thirty-one years old and with a five-year-old son and a four-year-old daughter, Dorothy, who worked for pay, knew well the burdens that a stressful job could impose on a mother. As a television producer, she worked in the very early morning hours. Since her husband was engaged in significant travel for his job, much of the child care work fell on Dorothy. One day she had an epiphany. She was exhausted most of the time and one afternoon after work dozed off at home. She awoke to the sounds of her daughter playing in the toilet bowl, an event that stirred in her a mother's greatest fear: her child's potential drowning. The next day she quit her job. Confronted by this prospect of life or death, she did not want any other mother to experience what she went through, and she viewed flexibility as offering all women the best possible options as they made the decision on engaging in paid work.

Workplace Flexibility as Helping Mothers Better Manage Their Work and Family Lives

Mothers who supported workplace flexibility as a galvanizing issue for a mothers' movement noted that such policies would enable all mothers to best manage their work and family lives. This was the second most commonly reported theme among this set of movement affirmers. Peggy, fifty-five and a MomsRising member, was no longer at a point in her life when she needed to be concerned about taking time off from work for her son, who was fourteen. However, she vividly remembered such worries when her son was younger.

> I think that definitely [we could build a mothers' movement around workplace flexibility because mothers are] always juggling, . . . And I remember that, too. It was just horrible trying to juggle [everything] when the kid was sick or doctors' appointments [that you had to attend to] and your own work needs.

As an architect and planner, Peggy considered herself "lucky" in her circumstances because at least as a salaried, professional worker, she did not need to document her absences as would an hourly employee. Shannon, too, observed the advantages that she had in caring for her four children, ages seven and under. As described earlier, she was a thirty-five-year-old member of MomsRising. Shannon recognized and appreciated the flexible policies she was able to obtain that other mothers simply do not have.

> I think that if women just spent time with each other, they would see that we have a lot more in common than we [thought]. . . . We are going to support the choices they make no matter what, and if they

know that, then they won't be afraid to speak up about . . . why they need flexibility in their schedules. . . . They need maybe a little bit of leave. [My employer] let me use my sick leave to take time off to get my children the H1N1 flu shot. . . . I know many mothers who can't do that. . . . I am going to take the whole day off and stand in line to get my kids' flu shots. So what does that mean for women who don't have sick leave, who have to go to work because they don't have the leave to stand in line to get the kids' flu shots?

As noted earlier, Sharon was a state employee in human services. She was particularly attuned to these issues because at various stages in her career, she had worked under different supervisors who allowed her more or less flexibility. Earlier in her career working for the state, a supervisor permitted her to have flexible hours, which was critically important to her in attending to the needs of her two older children. These children had previously been in foster care; and had therapy appointments for behavioral and emotional difficulties, appointments that took place during the day. This supervisor retired, and Sharon's new boss did not allow this type of flexibility. When Sharon was under this more restrictive regime, she felt truly constrained in taking care of her children and felt as if their well-being suffered as a result.

According to many mothers' group members, gender disparities in child care responsibilities make it much more likely that women rather than men will come together on the workplace flexibility issue. At twenty-six years old, a young mother of two children, and a Mocha Moms member, Cynthia echoed Peggy and Shannon's belief that having access to flexibility would be of critical help for mothers, as they are the ones who usually need to bring their children to medical appointments.

Even if moms are working, the majority of tasks like that fall on them. You know, so, yeah, it would make [life] a lot easier. You could say, "Could I have an extended lunch break?" Or, "I need an hour and I'll make it up somewhere else." I think that would be a great thing.

Since the bulk of caregiving work still falls on mothers rather than fathers, workplace flexibility would definitely help mothers manage the daily activities they need to get through. But there might be an even more important benefit, one that would go far in achieving gender equality in caregiving. According to this perspective, if these policies were promoted among *all* workers, including men, perhaps fathers would actually utilize them and do more to contribute to the family's well-being. According to Jada, identified earlier, thirty-one, a member of Mothers & More, and the mother of a two-year-old son, mothers and fathers need to learn to work more cooperatively as a team in raising their children, and workplace flexibility policies would afford such possibilities.

> Why are we making it so impossible for moms to have a life outside of their children when it's been proven time and time again that mothers who have lives outside of their children are better mothers? I feel like that's something [policy makers] need to start focusing on and realizing that just because a mom, you know, wants to work or a mom wants to go out at night, that that doesn't make her a bad mother. It actually makes her a better mother. . . . That even extends to husbands because I think . . . that when you give the husbands or the dads more leeway in their jobs, that takes the pressure off of the moms being the only people who can take care of things. . . . I just feel like, you know, more pressure needs to be taken off of mothers.

In her current job, as noted earlier, Jada took customer service calls that were routed to her home. This afforded her quite a bit of flexibility in her job. However, she also worked in different environments, such as at a grocery store, where she had little to no flexibility. Overall, then, her ability to have more options in working while taking care of her son, as well as her strong desire that men play a more responsible role in the flexibility debate by actually assuming more care responsibilities, motivated her to support the development of a strong mothers' movement around this issue.

Flexibility would also enable mothers to lead happier lives in the opinion of mothers' group members, especially those mothers with a strong proclivity for paid work. Rita, thirty-one and a MomsRising member, as described earlier, had a four-year-old daughter and one-year-old son. In her view, most mothers who give up their careers do not want to do so but are forced out by the inflexible nature of their jobs. To remedy this situation, the United States needs to model its flexibility policies on those currently in place in Europe and elsewhere. As scholars have noted, other countries have an integrated system of paid maternity leave, paid sick days, strong protections for part-time work, active pre-school programs, and after-school care that help mothers manage their time in ways that Americans can only dream about.[6] Rita stated:

> [We need to just make] institutional changes to make work more flex-ible and also have . . . structural help for things like day care and sick care. [We need after-school] care when school is out just to make it more possible for women to work. Then [we need] increases in all sorts of leaves like maternity leave. . . . [We need policies] here [where] women can have one foot in the workforce and one foot at home so that they can transition much more easily when the child is full time at home [and then moves onto] school. . . . There are models in Europe, all over the place, where it is possible and women transition a lot more seamlessly than we do.

Echoing the sentiments of many other mothers in the study, Rita noted how fortunate she was that she did not have to make the difficult choice forced on some women between paid work and taking care of their children. As an adjunct professor at a local university, she had con-siderable flexibility in scheduling her work hours. Yet around her she saw women, especially high-achieving women, struggling and wanted to be part of a strong form of collective action to address and conquer the stress that at times overwhelmed them.

Workplace Flexibility as Not Strong Enough to Build a Movement

The minority of mothers who disagreed that workplace flexibility was a compelling enough issue around which to build a movement tended to focus on one central theme: that the issue did not have enough impor-tance to be a uniting force among different types of mothers. Crystal, mentioned earlier, was fifty-two and a Mothers & More member with two daughters, ages ten and five, at home. She was blunt in making the following argument:

> I do not think [workplace flexibility] is a strong enough issue. . . . When faced with the things to do with your children or your children's

future, especially not just your day-to-day caring for your children, but big issues, societal issues, cultural issues for your children's future—these are much bigger than workplace flexibility.

In this statement, Crystal made it clear that she believed that workplace flexibility issues were less important than other areas of public policy that concerned her as a parent. In a similar way, Lisa, a thirty-six-year-old mother of a four-year-old son, and a Mocha Moms member, asserted that she, too, was not against mothers coming together on behalf of a significant cause. However, while some employment issues might rise to that level, workplace flexibility did not.

I don't think that there is a consensus there because I mean, what jobs are you talking about [that deserve to be flexible]? You have got to kind of earn it, too. It just doesn't seem like you should just get it. You have got to show that you are a good employee. I don't know. I guess there needs to be some consensus around the fact that women should not lose their jobs more often than men because of issues unrelated to their work performance. That is an issue [that I care about] but I do not think the issue of more flexibility . . . is necessarily . . . a national issue.

On the one hand, blatant gender discrimination in the workplace in hiring and firing was for Lisa a significant concern that should be addressed through policy solutions, and she was willing to commit personal resources toward fighting that fight. On the other hand, workplace flexibility, in her view, should be determined on a case-by-case basis and definitely was not something women deserved as a right. Her perspective was intriguing, given her work history. As a reporter covering Capitol Hill for a period, she had worked for demanding bosses who expected her to be available for assignments at all times. When she left that job to work as a financial reporter, her employer once again expected a lot of her in terms of travel with very little advanced notice. Perhaps the fact that she had only one child and a very supportive husband made her feel as if flexibility policies were not necessarily critical issues for mothers more generally.

Rebecca echoed this theme when she reflected back on her own work history. A NAMC member, at twenty-six she had an eighteen-month-old daughter. While she did not unfavorably compare workplace flexibility with other national issues that needed attention, as did Crystal and Lisa, she did think of it much more narrowly in scope.

> I just don't see flexibility as being a major [issue]. . . . But I think if a company started needing people, and it offered flexibility as an incentive, I think [it] could get a lot of very intelligent women into the job force who may not have otherwise gotten into the job force. But again, that [should be] on the company's [initiative], not on moms pushing flexibility. . . . I don't think I've met moms who aren't working because their jobs didn't offer enough flexibility.

Rebecca came to this conclusion as a result of her personal experiences. When she was pregnant with her daughter, she decided to leave her job as a receptionist for a prestigious symphony. In her interview, she commented that no amount of flexibility would have changed her mind about her wanting to stay at home with her daughter. She reasoned that most probably felt the same way as she did, thereby reducing the issue of flexibility as one of national significance in her mind.

While the preceding set of mothers did not see workplace flexibility as rising to the level of issues on which they wanted to focus their energies, other mothers agreed that it was important but emphasized that the main barrier to mobilization was encouraging women in different circumstances to unite in advocating for change. For Kristin, thirty-one, a MomsRising member, and the mother of a seven-year-old girl and a three-year-old boy, the main difficulty was encouraging stay-at-home mothers to view the issue as being essential to their well-being, as much as do mothers who are currently working for pay. Although, as demonstrated in chapter 5, *both* groups of mothers valued these options, Kristin feared that mothers' current work statuses could be an obstacle to all sides rallying together.

> I would still say there are divisions there. I mean, I can honestly hear the banter of, Well, . . . you made the decision to work and not stay at home, so now you are asking for rights or additional [privileges] or whatever the case may be? So, I don't know. Could working moms unite over [workplace flexibility]? Yes, certainly. I don't know that *all* moms could.

As Kristin focused on the problems of bridging the interests of mothers who stay at home and mothers who work for pay, she worried about those who wanted flexibility as a matter of right. On this point, she noted that a certain segment of the population would always argue that everyone should be treated equally, with flexibility being a "bonus" rather than a required feature of a standard job in the competitive American economy.

Members of mothers' organizations clearly had much to say when it came to reflecting on their participation in a broader mothers' movement. According to the survey data, about two-thirds of these members did not believe that they are participating in a larger enterprise than their own group. Instead, as detailed in the interview data, they viewed their organizations as places that mostly help them with the everyday tasks of raising their children. Interestingly, this is what they often wanted from their groups, or alternatively, solely what the groups seemed to be offering them. Mothers who *did* believe that they are participating in such a movement right now offered a variety of reasons for their beliefs. These included the idea that through their group, they believed that they are helping to redefine the meaning of motherhood, educating others in solving common motherhood problems, and advocating on behalf of mothers' issues across the country.

While only a minority of group members believed that they are part of a mothers' movement right now, they had a completely different perspective on whether a mothers' movement should exist in the future. In considering this question, two-thirds of survey participants agreed that mothers should be mobilized. Moreover, according to both the survey and interviews, these mothers rated workplace flexibility as *the* potentially unifying issue around which to bring women together. In effect, they were directly at odds with the minority of mothers who maintained that the issue simply was not an important enough priority in American politics or was too divisive in the population at large. Mothers promoting the more positive perspective argued that workplace flexibility would assist all mothers in making paid work decisions and also help them better manage their work and family lives.

For advocates of workplace flexibility, then, this chapter ends with a note of hope. Significant numbers of women in mothers' groups do desire to come together to form a mothers' movement. Moreover, they believe that resolving the conflicts between work and family that plague them in their current lives should be the focal point of such a movement. How then, should these mothers craft such a mobilization effort? What steps would be necessary for them to achieve the political momentum that they need to obtain these much desired reforms?

7

Mothers Need Leadership, Too

We've come here today to have a conversation about workplace flexibility: an important part of balancing our responsibilities as employees, as breadwinners, mothers, fathers, sons, daughters, husbands, and wives.

It's an issue that many folks have struggled with for so many years, and one that we as a society just haven't really quite figured out yet.

And as the parents of two beautiful young daughters, it is an issue that is particularly important to me and my husband, as you know. . . . I've talked about this so often.

And it is true, in our current life, we are incredibly blessed. We have amazing resources and support systems here at the White House that I could have never imagined. Number one of them is having Grandmother living upstairs. We all need one of those. So can you figure that out?

But we didn't always live in the White House. And for many years before coming to Washington, I was a working mother, doing my best to juggle the demands of my job with the needs of my family, with a husband who has crazy ideas.

And as I've said before, I consider myself, as many of us in this room do, as a 120-percenter, which means that if I'm not doing something at 120 percent, I feel like I'm failing. And I know you all can relate to that. So while I did the best that I could at work and at home, I felt like I wasn't keeping up with either one of them enough.

And I was lucky—I had understanding bosses, I had very accom-modating jobs. In fact, in the last job I had before coming to the White House—I remember this clearly—I was on maternity leave with Sasha, still trying to figure out what to do with my life, and I got a call for an interview for this position, a senior position at the hospitals. And I thought, okay, here we go. So I had to scramble to look for [a baby-sitter], and couldn't find one. So what did I do? I packed up that little infant, and I put her in the stroller, and I brought her with me. And I prayed that her presence wouldn't be an automatic disqualifier. And it was fortunate for me that, number one, she slept through the entire interview. And I was still breastfeeding—if that's not too much infor-mation. And I got the job.

But I know that I was lucky, number one. I was interviewing with the president that had just had a child himself and was very understand-ing and open-minded. But I know that most folks are nowhere near as lucky as I was. Particularly right now with the job market the way it is, many folks can't afford to be picky about the jobs that they take. Many folks don't have access to any kind of family leave policies whatsoever. No flexible working arrangements. Many people don't even have a paid sick day. So they are struggling—struggling every day to find affordable childcare; or someone to look after an aging parent, which is becoming more the issue; scrambling to make things work when the usual ar-rangements fall through. All of us have been through that.

So they spend a lot of time hoping and praying that everything will work out just perfectly. I remember those days, just the delicate bal-ance of perfection. And as all the parents in this room know, it's never perfect—ever.

But here's the thing: As we all know here today, it just doesn't have to be that way, doesn't have to be that hard. And that's something that I learned for myself, not just as an employee but as a manager, when I discovered that the more flexibility that I gave to my staff to be good parents, and I valued that, the happier my staff was likely to be and the greater chance they were to stay and not leave, because they knew they might not find the same kind of flexibility somewhere else.[1]

—First Lady Michelle Obama, March 31, 2010

At the historic first White House Forum on Workplace Flexibility in 2010, First Lady Michelle Obama brought her own personal struggles of balancing work and family once again into the limelight of national politics. Since she and her husband confront the challenges of these issues daily, she felt particularly drawn and even compelled to move their private discussions about these matters into the public forum. The conference brought together people with different perspectives on these issues, including business leaders, labor organizers, academic experts, and even the president himself. The commonality that they all had was a keen interest in exchanging ideas on how workplace flexibility initiatives can be adopted by large and small firms alike, across the maximum number of industries, and for the benefit of workers across the income spectrum.

In many ways, this book has been about the foundation for what is ultimately needed in advancing the cause of workplace flexibility. The bricks that compose the foundation are already in place. Five strong mothers' organizations exist today with thousands of members located across the country. They all have an online presence, and four out of the five hold meetings where members speak about the issues that are important to them, face to face, on a regular basis. These topics of conversation range from the sharing of emotions involved in adult friendship to keeping up with activity ideas for their children. Group members also engage in public policy discussions by creatively thinking about the ways in which their lives could be improved with the assistance of government.

Within this context, there are undoubtedly significant differences among these groups. MOPS members tend to focus on issues from a Christian perspective, while Mocha Moms addresses the needs of mothers of color. The NAMC uses a community-building perspective in solving motherhood problems, and Mothers & More emphasizes the fulfillment of its members as complete women, not just in their role as mothers. Finally, MomsRising is on the cutting edge of Internet organizing for a variety of issues affecting mothers today. Both across and within each of these groups, however, is a split that is perhaps deeper and more important than any other: the decision that each member makes about working for pay. Members who currently work for pay, versus members who stay at home, are clear about their circumstances and why they have made the arrangements they have implemented in their lives. As this book has demonstrated, at times each side may make judgments about the other, although, importantly, this negative dynamic was shown to be relatively rare.

Despite this diversity, there are strong signs of hope for unity. Most critically, in this study, across groups, and among both mothers currently working for pay and mothers staying at home, there was an active interest in creating a world with more flexibility. For mothers working for pay, this would mean greater opportunities to balance their work and family lives, which they could take advantage of immediately. And for mothers currently staying at home, these policies would enable them to think about the ways in which they could return to paid work most effectively, if they so choose.

These groups and their members' beliefs and sense of community all provide the basis for a mothers' movement grounded in workplace flexibility in the United States. Workplace flexibility *can* unite mothers across the country. What is needed now is strong leadership in moving forward. The first component of this leadership must come in the form of concrete policy ideas. By hosting the White House Forum on Workplace Flexibility, Michelle Obama and like-minded organizers aimed to shine a national spotlight on the ways in which industry and the government alike can cooperate to create additional opportunities for all workforce participants. Symbolically through this event, what was once a "private issue" that individual families had to resolve on their own was on the presidential radar screen with the aim of encouraging bold new innovations in this area. The second component of leadership that is needed is more effective group mobilization to pursue these goals. While the different groups studied here have distinct approaches to workplace flexibility and how it can be encouraged among employers, effectively harnessing their collective energy is central to the realization of enhanced employment opportunities for mothers everywhere.

Component 1: Leadership in Policy Ideas

As demonstrated in chapter 5, there is clearly a strong level of support for government intervention in promoting workplace flexibility. However, different forms of intervention received different levels of approval among mothers' group members. Matching these levels of support with appropriate public policies is crucial as mothers forge ahead on developing a plan of attack on these issues. Consider each of the public policies analyzed by mothers' group members here, and what, if anything, can and should be done to achieve them.

1. The government should educate employers and employees about the benefits of flexible work arrangements and best practices regarding how to implement flexible work arrangements.

Education on best practices and workplace flexibility was by far one of the most popular ways mothers' group members and those across the paid work divide believed that workplace flexibility could be achieved in the United States today. According to this view, many potentially enthusiastic employers simply may not know the best way to go about implementing flexible work policies for their particular employees. Alternatively, employers are just used to traditional ways of doing business and find it challenging to alter their standard operating procedures to explore workplace flexibility options.

If either is the case, the government can get involved in various ways to promote workplace flexibility. First, it can do a better job of disseminating best practices to those firms that might be on the cusp of doing more but have not yet taken concrete steps in that direction. This could be accomplished using a multitude of methods, such as the different levels of government becoming more engaged in publicizing websites that feature best practices, distributing printed materials, and creating and uploading videos to key business-related sites on the Internet. But this can also be done through leading by example. For instance, the federal government has been a key innovator in the area of telecommuting since the 1970s and early 1980s when small pilot programs began operating in select agencies such as the Internal Revenue Service, the Railroad Retirement Board, the National Aeronautic and Space Administration, the Department of Labor, and the General Services Administration.[2] Later, in 1989, the Flexiplace pilot program began, which focused on promoting work-at-home opportunities across a wider range of agencies within the federal government. Federal telecommuting centers furnished with professional, up-to-date work equipment began sprouting up across the country in 1993, and by 1996, the administration of President Bill Clinton set in motion the National Telecommuting Initiative, which articulated ambitious targets for encouraging more government workers to telework. Presidents George W. Bush and

Barack Obama continued efforts to move federal workers forward in this direction by encouraging more of them to work (for example, through the Telework Enhancement Act of 2010), whenever possible, from home. At the state level, innovation is also evident. For example, North Carolina has directed its government agencies to promote telework among state employees, and Arizona has required that its offices establish travel reduction programs, which may involve, for instance, educating workers about telecommuting. Other state and local governments should also be encouraged to become innovators for their employees as well.

Second, all levels of government can facilitate technical assistance for companies that want to do more for their workers in this area but do not as of yet have the nuts-and-bolts knowledge of how to do so. This can be accomplished through government or private company–supplied instructional materials, as described above. Most important, this technical assistance should be directed at a variety of audiences. Employers, for example, should be able to learn under what conditions flexibility might be helpful to them and how ultimately to implement such policies. Human resources departments should be able to understand the ways in which such policies are best put into practice in a fair and equitable manner. And last, employees should be able to process how to design such requests in ways that are beneficial to both themselves and the organizations for which they work.[3]

2. The government should encourage employers to voluntarily increase access to flexible work arrangements, by, for example, providing grants, awards, and tax incentives.

Equally supported by mothers' group members and across the paid work divide was the idea that the government should become more actively involved in encouraging flexibility through a variety of concrete financial measures. Grants and awards give businesses the financial backing that they need to innovate, especially in labor force issues that might traditionally be seen as risky. In motivating them to take these steps forward, the federal government as well as the states and localities could become more invested in promoting innovation through competitions in the flexible work arena. This might involve, for example, issuing monetary bonuses and prizes to those organizations establishing cutting-edge practices affecting the most workers, or distributing awards to groups that are otherwise changing the landscape of worker well-being in dynamic and novel ways.

Tax incentives also provide companies with the budgetary room that they might need to pursue flexibility policies in an innovative direction. Right now, most of these initiatives are taking place at the state level. For example, Virginia offers businesses up to fifty thousand dollars in tax incentives and reimbursements related to the purchase of telecommuting items such as laptops, Internet access services, computer peripherals, and the like. A recent law added a twelve-hundred-dollar tax credit per employee for businesses taking these steps.[4] Georgia offers the same types of bonuses as Virginia, providing up to twenty thousand dollars per business, plus a tax credit of twelve hundred dollars per employee for such initiatives in certain prespecified industries, such as manufacturing, light industrial construction, research and development, and tourism.[5]

Similar federal efforts would clearly help move flexibility forward by establishing the national government as a key player in this area and potentially even as a leader for the remaining other states to follow in developing their own programs. In the 112th Congress, a bill titled the Telework Tax Incentive Act (H.R. 710, with a previous version introduced in 2009) proposed to amend the Internal Revenue Service code to provide employers or employees with a tax credit of up to one thousand dollars a year for purchases of telecommuting-related equipment. Although not likely to move forward immediately, this legislation provides the blueprint for future federal efforts in establishing a clear signal for many organizations to follow in the adoption of more flexibility options.

3. The government should require employers to establish a process under which employees can request flexible work arrangements and employers must consider those requests.

4. The government should require employers to grant a certain number of requests for flexible work arrangements per year.

Mothers' group members and those mothers across the paid work divide were more hesitant to support policies that mandated that firms and other organizations actually engage in certain workplace flexibility practices, especially ones that would require employers to grant flexible work arrangements every year. Reflective of this sentiment, while paid sick day initiatives were passed in localities such as San Francisco in 2006; Washington, DC, and Milwaukee in 2008; and Connecticut in 2011, in the federal government, both Senate and House versions of a bill containing similar provisions have stalled since an initial version was introduced in 2004. The most recently proposed legislation, called the Healthy Families Act (H.R. 1875 and S. 984 in the 112th Congress), would require that employers with fifteen or more employees give their workers seven paid sick days per year. This legislation also would allow workers time to recover from their own illnesses or trauma, such as domestic violence, or use the time to take care of loved ones. Another idea that has been introduced in the 112th Congress, in the House of Representatives but without Senate action yet, is the Federal Employees Paid Parental Leave Act (H.R. 616), which would offer federal employees paid leave for four out of their twelve weeks of guaranteed coverage under the Family and Medical Leave Act. A version of this was originally introduced in 2000 and still has not made progress through the congressional hearing process. With hesitancy so far over ideas that involve such mandates, policy leaders must be aware that these two ideas, employees' right to request flexibility and their right to actually receive any type of flexibility, might take time to mature within the American political system. Nevertheless, there are models in European countries for how this could work in the United States that would impose minimal burdens on employers.

In 2002, for example, the United Kingdom adopted a law giving employees the right to request a flexible work arrangement if they have children under the age of six (or eighteen if that child has a disability).[6] It is up to the employee to make the request in writing to the employer and explain its potential impact on the workplace environment. The two sides then must meet in person within a designated time frame (twenty-eight days) to discuss this proposed arrangement and then the employer must make a decision within fourteen days. Notably, the employer has a wide range of reasons under which he or she can legally deny these claims, and employees can appeal decisions only based on improper procedures being followed, not on the business-related justification presented by the employer for the denial.

It is important to emphasize that this law does not require that employers provide any type of workplace flexibility options—simply that they have processes in place to hear these requests. Even so, while employees might immediately see the benefit in having these policies, businesses have many concerns to consider as they review these queries. They have to keep their companies profitable, with stable employees ready and able to do the work that is necessary for meeting the employers' strategic objectives. They might worry about fraud and abuse, as well as unnecessary paperwork and lawsuits, in implementing these types of laws. Policy leaders in the United States therefore might be wise to move to initiatives in these areas slowly, perhaps through the use of pilot programs with the federal government and other interested private companies.

Overall, government leadership can clearly be proactive in each of the four issue domains described above. However, leadership is also necessary in removing the *fear* that many employers and employees have in seeking workplace flexibility. Employers, for example, may be apprehensive about violating the National Labor Standards Act in its provisions granting labor's right to determine certain conditions of work. More specifically, the Fair Labor Standards Act requires time-and-a-half pay for those working more than forty hours a week. Certain types of compressed workweeks with overload schedules one week and reduced schedules the next might trigger this time-and-a-half requirement, which employers might be hesitant to pay. Employees face another set of issues. Those who live and work in one state while their employers are located in another state might face double income taxation. Moreover, individuals might not be able to work reduced hours and collect retirement benefits under certain plans, as regulated by the Employee Retirement Income Security Act and the Internal Revenue Service. While some of these employer and employee issues may simply require clarification from federal and state authorities in the proper application of relevant laws and rules, other concerns may need further legislation in order to be fully addressed.[7]

Component 2: Leadership in Group Mobilization

Leadership in policy ideas is clearly important, and a significant array of proposals have emerged to help address some of the key workplace flexibility initiatives considered here. But every good set of ideas must be followed by political action in the form of a mobilized front of citizens seriously pushing for reform. How can the mothers' groups described here—as well as their potential allies—best march forward in this direction? Five steps are clearly necessary.

The most important finding generated from this book is that there is significant support for the proliferation of workplace flexibility options; even mothers who currently stay at home are looking toward a future that might involve paid employment. But before that, as the survey and interview data show, these groups together, along with their like-minded organizational friends, need to see that they are fighting for a common cause that can form the backbone of an important and powerful social movement. This, the first step, is not as simple as it seems. After all, as described throughout this book, these groups *do* come to the flexibility issue with divergent identities. Mocha Moms, for example, focuses on the needs of mothers of color, while MOPS strives to serve Christian mothers. With these distinct constituencies, could it be the case that such groups will always be balkanized, prevented from acting in concert?

The data presented in this book argue against this outcome. In fact, although they might have individual identities, along the continuum of their paid-work–stay-at-home memberships, these groups can tap into a unified set of activists. Clearly, for those groups with more mothers working for pay, flexible work arrangements can help them achieve their goals of fostering the best possible outcomes for their children. In addition, work tasks can be more effectively completed if mothers know that their children are being taken care of properly and at the appropriate times. For those groups with more mothers who stay at home, flexible work arrangements can be framed in the same way. If they appreciate that the modern workplace encourages hands-on parenting in the form of flexible work options for mothers who either want to or have to work for pay, these groups will surely assess this new business model as pro-family and as a boon for accomplishing the many tasks of motherhood.

Once they recognize their commonalities, all the groups can then begin to extend their reach beyond their registered members to others who might be interested in these issues. MomsRising, for example, uses Twitter and Facebook to establish connections with concerned mothers beyond its membership. Besides using social media,

MomsRising works with over 150 affiliated organizations, such as the AFL-CIO and the Center for Law and Social Policy, to promote changes in the public policy landscape. Such organizations typically share the workplace vision of MomsRising and can help the group reach potentially like-minded mothers. NAMC has moved in a similar direction, developing regularly updated blogs and webinars on topics important to both its members and the larger public. MOPS, Mocha Moms, and Mothers & More have been pursuing some initiatives here as well, but many of their activities are still restricted to members. In terms of other forms of alliance building, all these groups need to recognize that even their more conservative members share their interest in workplace flexibility. Therefore, conversations with all types of outside groups—including business and family-focused organizations—are clearly necessary to advance the cause of workplace flexibility.

What about a stronger alliance with labor unions, which MomsRising has already initiated in its partnership with the AFL-CIO, referred to above? Undoubtedly, unions have long been on the decline in the United States. With its diminished representation of workers has come a loss of influence in transforming work culture. In addition, unions have been somewhat reluctant to assume a leading role on issues such as flexible work schedules that might apply to only a smaller segment of the workers they represent.[8] Instead, they have focused attention on policies that can be equally applied to all workers, such as child care and health care. However, if union members so desired, they could perhaps redirect their leaders to work more actively on behalf of a broader range of flexibility issues. The main question for mothers' groups, it seems, is whether additional alliances with unions would be viewed either positively or negatively in the eyes of their own members. Recent research into how Americans view unions argues that they retain support among the general population but that this support sometimes hovers around 50 percent and can vary year to year.[9] Given the diversity of political views across mothers' groups, building strong and visible partnerships with unions might not be the most efficacious way to move forward on the issue of workplace flexibility.

While the case for working with labor unions is somewhat undetermined, there is one set of allies that mothers' groups *must* approach if they hope and expect to effect change. That group, of course, is men. Even if all employers were to offer maximum flexibility for their employees, mothers would still face a multitude of problems without a fundamental restructuring of family responsibilities, for which they still shoulder the burden of tasks. This is true because even when flexibility is available to employees, it does not always mean that women end up doing less household work and child care.[10] Numerous studies have explored the impact of flexibility options such as shift work and alternative work locations and have found mixed results in their ability to free up time for women.[11] In other words, with these flexibility options in place, mothers occasionally use the available time to do *more* household and child care tasks. Further, given the unequal division between the sexes in who assumes responsibilities in the home, mothers continue to pay a price for even participating in the labor force. Most well known is that they face discrimination in pay.[12] But beyond the issue of pay differentials, mothers, compared with nonmothers, are less likely to be hired, more likely to be perceived negatively on the job, and more likely to be evaluated poorly when opportunities for advancement occur.[13] In isolation, no amount of workplace flexibility options will solve these issues. Rather, men must accelerate their pace of equal engagement in child care and household responsibilities, such that flexibility can have real and meaningful impacts in multiple areas of all workers' lives. In sum, *mothers' duties* must be redefined as *parental duties*. Indeed, there is cause for optimism, as younger generations of men do appear to be increasingly espousing these types of egalitarian principles.[14]

In the second step to reform, these groups need to develop and emphasize common pathways for achieving the type of open, flexible workplace they desire. On this point, in this book I not only probed levels of support for workplace flexibility initiatives but also asked respondents about what kinds of public policy initiatives they would endorse to achieve implementation of their ideas. While governmental initiatives mandating that employers offer flexibility itself did not receive widespread support, other policies received overwhelming or at least majority approval across a plurality of groups, and across mothers who stay at home as well as mothers who work for pay. As reiterated in this chapter, these policies included the government's offering to educate businesses about the importance of flexibility; providing firms with awards, grants, and incentives to promote flexibility; and even requiring companies to establish a process whereby they would at least consider employees' requests for such options. Further, while not directly investigated in this study, flexibility options in the United States are frequently generated by businesses themselves, without government intervention. Because such corporate initiatives do not involve the potentially more contentious issue of government involvement in the economy, they are likely to be popular among members of all mothers' groups. In its totality, then, this book has demonstrated that mothers' groups can and should stress their shared perspective on the appropriate role of government and businesses themselves in encouraging workplace flexibility.

The third step to reform entails that mother's groups do a better job in diversifying their core membership. As demonstrated throughout this book, the majority of members in mothers' groups are middle- and upper-middle-class heterosexual women. They are also predominantly married, and with the exception of Mocha Moms, mostly white. This lack of diversity can create numerous problems for the cause of workplace flexibility. Sociodemographic groups that are not yet part of the dominant mothers' group constituencies may fail to recognize how flexibility could benefit them and may resent the push for any changes to their work-family lives that they see benefitting others rather than themselves. Even worse, employers might recognize such divisions and refuse to introduce any flexibility measures, with the justification that only "special interests" want them.

Perhaps the most difficult set of mothers to attract into the ranks of mothers' groups are working-class and low-income mothers. This is not necessarily an inherent failing of the groups themselves. Frequently, mothers on the lower levels of the socioeconomic scale simply do not have the time or resources to join mothers' groups. They must focus on meeting their families' immediate financial needs. It is also the case, however, that their priorities in workplace flexibility options might be completely different from those of existing group members. When it comes to many hourly wage jobs, firms often prefer to retain workers who have "open availability" and can switch their work hours or reduce them on a week-to-week basis. While this helps businesses meet the exigencies of supply and demand, mothers, who must be ready to take care of their children on a predictable schedule, are less likely to be this flexible.[15] Low-income mothers have criticized similar employer policies, including those regarding night shifts and mandatory overtime, that place heavy burdens on them in terms of coordinating care for their children. Add these concerns to the high cost of child care and the lack of paid sick leave, and women at the lower end of the socioeconomic spectrum confront an almost hostile working environment on a daily basis.[16] Right now, these types of flexibility issues have been given less priority by mothers' groups than the more middle-class issues of flexible starting or stopping times and paths toward career acceleration or deceleration. However, in order to build an effective movement that draws on the maximum array of experiences of women across the board, all these groups need to do a better job of meeting the needs of broader classes of mothers.

Commendably, mothers' groups have been taking steps in the right direction. The mission statements and objectives of all of these groups certainly promote membership inclusivity across a wide range of sociodemographic characteristics. Mothers & More, for example, emphasizes on its website that its "members are women of all ages, with children of all ages." MOPS opens its doors to mothers working for pay and those not working for pay and extends its outreach by creating specialized military, teen, and Spanish-speaking chapters. Mocha Moms states that it is dedicated to women of all races and work statuses, and it explicitly does not discriminate against mothers based on ethnicity, sex, gender, socioeconomic level, education, or religion. Finally, both the NAMC and MomsRising make it clear throughout their websites that mothers from any background are welcome to be a part of their cause.

Despite these public proclamations about desiring more diversity, however, clearly much more must be done to achieve this goal. MomsRising is a shining example in this regard. Beginning in 2008, MomsRising started placing greater emphasis on issues that have wider appeal to racial minorities and those experiencing financial vulnerability. These issues include paid family leave, paid sick days, family economic security, and ending hiring and wage discrimination against mothers of color. In addition, the group began seeking out partnerships with the Labor Council on Latin American Advancement; the Asian American Center for Advancing Justice's Conference on Advancing Activists; the Blogging While Brown Conference; the Immigration, Faith and Labor Roundtable; and the National Korean American Service and Education Consortium. Further, MomsRising has energetically encouraged women of color to post on its website. The other organizations studied in this book would do well to follow suit in these types of out-reach and recruiting efforts.

For the fourth step to reform, these groups need to demonstrate leadership in marketing their workplace flexibility goals to their own membership. While MOPS does not have a strong explicit statement about workplace flexibility on its website, it does promote the idea that all mothers should achieve their fullest potential, whatever that may be, including working for pay. All the other groups in this study make clear statements about supporting workplace flexibility goals, although they might disagree about how to achieve them. Nevertheless, as data from both the survey and the interviews showed, members are not al-ways aware of or mobilized by these goals. Frequently, they come to the groups seeking friendship and support, and organizational projects be-yond these interests may remain less visible to them. The groups thus need to do a much better job of highlighting the workplace flexibility issue as central to their missions. This could be done not only through online communications but also via chapter-based, face-to-face educa-tion where appropriate as well.

The fifth and final step to reform highlights that these groups need to engage much more vigorously in promoting their members' identifi-cation with a larger mothers' movement that directly prioritizes work-place flexibility. Beyond simply offering members information about workplace flexibility, there are specific, critical steps that these groups can take to encourage their members to see the work-family difficulties they experience in their own lives as part of a pattern that runs deeper than their own personal frustrations. The first action to consider is re-forming the ways in which these groups offer their members benefits. There is some evidence that certain types of organizations with impor-tant public policy goals can suffer when they place too much empha-sis on providing their members with "personal services." For example, organizations that work against driving while intoxicated may offer victim aid assistance to families, and those advocating for improved maternal health care may subsidize individualized interventions aimed at reducing repeated hospitalizations.[17] By offering individuals such per-sonal services, which on the surface are extremely helpful, the groups paradoxically may be reducing their chances of attaining their broader, political goals. That is, members might become more consumed with getting their personal needs met instead of looking outward to demand more sweeping societal change. Mothers' groups, which provide a host of individual services, among them fellowship and emotional support for their members, may be falling prey to this same dilemma. As a result, member attachment to the group fails to translate into attachment to a broader mothers' movement.[18]

To overcome this potential problem, groups can help their members engage in a specific type of "identity work," or the activities in which individuals engage to give their lives meaning through their organizational affiliations.[19] Scholars have noted that there are two forms of identity work: one that is likely to build allegiance to the group by itself and is internal in nature, and another that is more likely to build solidarity to the movement overall and that is external in nature. Identity work that focuses solely on the group and is internal in nature aims to bring members closer together only with their own particular organization. The emphasis here is on establishing norms that distinguish group members from those outside the group. Common examples of internal identity work that groups might promote include the development of mission statements, core principles, services, formal goals, songs, rituals, and induction ceremonies to which outsiders cannot gain access.

In contrast, identity work that is external in nature focuses not on solidifying members' relationships to their own particular groups but on cementing their attachments to the movement overall on behalf of which they are fighting.[20] Groups that create more of a movement orientation encourage their members to become involved in other forms of engagement beyond their own organizations' boundaries, even if it requires a significant amount of effort. Indeed, it may be the case that the harder members work in their overall engagement with the broader social issues at stake, the more they become vested in the movement's success.[21]

Three pivotal forms of externally oriented identity work for members entail joining multiple groups, becoming involved in group recruitment efforts, and actively engaging in naming movement opponents. First, groups that want to foster a social movement can and should encourage their members to join a variety of organizations dedicated to the cause of workplace flexibility.[22] As additional groups gain larger memberships, they become more powerful and can work together to more effectively promote social change. Second, groups should advocate that their own members aggressively recruit others to participate in the cause they are seeking to advance. This can involve, for example, actively locating individuals in similar circumstances and encouraging them to be a part of the movement's political efforts. This system of recruitment is also essential to the movement-building process as it teaches individuals to tell their own particular stories of social injustice to others and relate them to more wide-ranging problems facing society.[23] Through the powerful process of relaying the details of one's personal struggles to potentially interested parties, individuals become more committed to helping others overcome the same barriers. In addition, through the retelling of their own narratives, they can become inspirational to outside observers and turn them into dedicated activists as well. Third, groups need to encourage their members to think about who might be opposing their efforts. By helping their members establish a strong sense of who is working against them, these groups will inevitably promote a stronger bond with their own movement overall.[24]

Conclusions

The media makes it clear that mothers have a lot to fight with one another about in contemporary American society. Should babies be breastfed or bottle fed? Should children be in public school or private school? Should they be homeschooled? What about sex education? How much should children receive, what should be the content, and when should they receive it? In how many structured activities should children be enrolled, and how much time should be unstructured? What kind of discipline is correct for each age group? What is the correct mix of praise versus constructive criticism for a child's behavior as she or he ages? What kind of medical attention and treatment is best when a child is ill? How should children receive religious instruction, if any? And perhaps most contentious of all, should mothers work for pay?—the classic Mommy Wars issue.

For all these debates over specific parenting issues, this book has been about something very different: consensus about the larger picture of mothering. True, the mothers here were affiliated with five different groups. They also came from an array of backgrounds related to their paid work status, with some staying at home, others working for pay part time, and others working for pay full time. Yet despite this diversity in group affiliations and paid work experiences, the mothers shared a strong goal: providing care for their children in the best way they saw fit.

Mothers across all the groups and across all levels of work engagement argued that the most effective manner in which they could accomplish this most important parenting goal involved the creation of a society that is more accommodating of the numerous demands that currently consume their lives. Significant numbers of mothers who work for pay and of mothers who stay at home expressed a strong desire for a proliferation of jobs that would afford them more flexible work arrangements; time-off options; and career exit, maintenance, and reentry opportunities. They joined arms in supporting various government initiatives to encourage businesses to promote such flexibility programs in the workplace.

Transforming public policy to move workplace flexibility forward will not by any means be easy. In both good and bad economic times, businesses will need to be convinced that such policies will benefit them over the long run in the key areas of organization, productivity, and most important, enhanced profitability. But so often in the past, employment options that most directly pertain to mothers have been thought of as automatically divisive and therefore politically untouchable. Mothers are too different from one another, the argument goes, to pursue such a transformation in employment practices. The analysis in this book has shown that when it comes to workplace flexibility, this simply is not true. Unity is the main story line here, and the mothers' groups outlined throughout the book have the potential to turn this issue into the foundation of a true mothers' movement, if new policy ideas and leadership for meaningful change can be effectively harnessed.

Appendix

Research Methodology

Interview Research Methodology

A. Recruitment, Nature of Participation, and Benefits from Involvement in Mothers' Group

1. Tell me about your current family situation. With whom do you live right now?
2. Tell me about your current paid work situation (full time, part time, or stay-at-home).
3. Walk me through your paid employment history, from the time you left high school until now. I want to know the kinds of jobs that you had, whether you worked part time or full time, and any gaps in your employment due to having children.
4. Did you ever talk with your husband (children's father) about his staying home? How was that decision made?
5. How did hear about your current mothers' group?
6. What made you decide to join this mothers' group?
7. What are the benefits that you receive from being a part of a group like this?
8. Have you tried to recruit other mothers that you know to join? If so, how do you do it?

9. What percentage of moms in your group work for pay versus stay at home?

10. What are the most common topics that come up for discussion in the group context?

B. *Challenges Presented by the Combination of Work and Family and Workplace Flexibility*

1. Let's talk about workplace flexibility, whether you are in the paid work force right now or not.

   I will list some workplace flexibility policies, and you tell me if you currently have these policies in place in your current job. If you are not currently working for pay right now, would you find any of these valuable if you decided to move back into the labor force? **For stay-at-home moms: Parts A and B, ask, Would these arrangements be *very important, somewhat important*, or *not important at all* in influencing your decision to go back to work? Part C, ask, Would this be a *high probability, medium probability*, or *low probability* that you would be able to return to your previous job or a similar job after a significant break of not working, such as more than one year?
   ** For mothers working for pay: Parts A and B, ask, Do you have *a lot of this type of flexibility, some of it*, or *none of it*? Part C, ask, Would this be a *high probability, medium probability*, or *low probability* that you would be able to return to your job or a similar job after a significant break of not working, such as more than one year?

   A. *Flexible work arrangements* (such as scheduling your hours, arranging overtime, deciding how many hours to work, deciding where to work)
   B. *Time off* (short-term time off, to attend a teacher's meeting, for example; recurring time off to handle a situation that comes up fairly predictably; or extended time off, meaning from five days to one year to take care of a baby, for example)
   C. *Easy exit and entry out of your job* (you can return to your job or a similar job after a significant break of not working, such as more than one year)

Depending on answers, ask if how having a lot (or a little) of this flexibility enables them to manage work and family or why it would help them to manage work and family. Ask for concrete examples.

2. Some people say that the government should promote workplace flexibility, through education, tax breaks, or laws. Other people say that the government should not be involved at all and employers should do this only if they want to. What do you think? Is this more the job of the government or employers?

3. Discrimination in the workplace for being a mother can mean many things.
   Here are some examples:

   A. During a job interview, you are asked about the number of children that you have, your pregnancy intention, or questions about who would take care of the kids while you are at work.
   B. Or maybe you were paid less than another worker without children, denied a promotion, or received a negative job evaluation because of your parenting responsibilities.

   Thinking about these examples, do you think that you were ever discriminated against in the workplace for being a mother or potentially becoming a mother?
   Get examples if possible.

4. Do you think discrimination against mothers in the workforce happens a lot, a little, or not so much? Why—from what others tell you, or the media? Get examples if possible.

5. Some people say that there is one ideal situation for almost all children and that ideal situation is that mothers should work for pay. Others say that the one ideal situation for almost all children is that mothers should stay at home. Do you think that there is one ideal situation for almost all children? If so, what is that arrangement? Why?

6. Is it ever hard to talk to your friends who are mothers and who have made different choices from yours regarding the balance of paid work and parenting in their lives? If so, why?

7. The media makes a huge deal out of the "Mommy Wars"—pitting mothers who work for pay versus stay-at-home mothers. Do you experience "Mommy Wars" among the people that you know, or do you think that this is more of a media creation?

8. Do you ever get angry or frustrated with your [husband, live-in partner, or men in general] with respect to their not doing enough to help raise the children? Tell me how you came to divide the child care responsibilities as to who does what in your household.

C. *Attitudes Toward Government, Political Behavior, and Political Ideology*

1. Tell me a bit about your political activities. Do you consider yourself a Republican, Democrat, or Independent? Do you vote regularly?

2. Tell me a bit about the history of your political activities. For example, do you work on behalf of causes that are important to you or give money to candidates running for office?

3. I would now like to ask you some questions about people who are running for Congress. Assuming that the following two candidates had the same qualifications and held the same policy positions, who in your mind would be most qualified to represent you in Congress: a stay-at-home mother or a mother who works for pay? Why?

4. Women's rights advocates can fight for a number of issues right now. Should women's rights advocates focus on policies that help mothers enter and find equality in the workforce, or should they do more for mothers in terms of raising their children, like fighting for larger tax breaks for dependent children? Why?

5. Many supporters of the women's movement called themselves feminists, but that label is less popular today. Do you consider yourself a feminist? Why or why not?

6. Do you think that you are part of a mothers' movement right now? Why or why not?

7. If there were to be a mothers' movement in the future, what issues do you think could build consensus or agreement? Would workplace flexibility be a unifying force? Why or why not?

Survey Research Methodology

The following was prepared by Marc D. Weiner, JD, PhD, assistant research professor, and associate director and faculty fellow, Bloustein Center for Survey Research, The Edward J. Bloustein School of Planning and Public Policy, Rutgers, The State University of New Jersey; for Jocelyn Elise Crowley, PhD, professor of public policy and principal investigator, The Edward J. Bloustein School of Planning and Public Policy, Rutgers, The State University of New Jersey.

The goal of this research is to explore the priorities of the organizational elite and rank-and-file memberships of five of the largest grassroots mothers' organizations in the United States. Using multimode research strategies, this study explores why mothers join these groups, especially as these reasons relate to their work-family concerns, and seeks to link those individual motivations to potential patterns of agreement on workplace flexibility issues across the membership of the groups.

This report presents a discussion of the survey research methodology for the Internet survey of the groups' rank-and-file members, followed by a discussion of the survey research methodology for the nationwide random sample telephone survey.

Internet Survey Population and Census and Sample Frames

The closed population for the Internet survey was the rank-and-file membership of five United States mothers' groups: NAMC, Mocha Moms, Mothers & More, MOPS, and MomsRising. The first task was to determine the survey eligibility of the members of each group, a process that started with each group's leadership providing the survey director with a gross set of presumptively unique membership records. That database was then pruned to remove the following non-unique records and nonrecords: duplicate records within groups, duplicate records across groups, and corrupt data proffered as records.

This first step resulted in a net set of unique membership records. That net set was then further pruned to remove those members not eligible for the survey because of failure to meet the survey qualification requirements; this included those members who had no chapter

TABLE A.1.
Internet survey census frames and sample frames derivations

	All groups	NAMC	Mocha Moms	Mothers & More	MOPS	MomsRising
Gross *N* records delivered	341,564	956	2,991	5,505	104,982	227,130
Duplicates, within groups	11,481	0	70	2	1,119	10,290
Duplicates, across groups	17	0	0	3	9	5
Corrupt records	11,085	0	0	45	0	11,040
Net *N* unique records delivered	318,981	956	2,921	5,455	103,854	205,795
Disqualifications						
No chapter affiliation	5,343	0	66	75	5,202	n/a
Not female	27,571	8	1	8	0	27,554
Not United States	2,082	0	0	0	1,241	841
Post sample delivery unsubscribes	3,758	0	0	0	0	3,758
Gross group population	280,227	948	2,854	5,372	97,411	173,642
Noncontactable/no valid e-mail address	17,775	63	1	28	12,827	4,856
Survey eligible/net group population	262,452	885	2,853	5,344	84,584	168,786
Census frames	9,082	885	2,853	5,344	n/a	n/a
Sample frames	10,000	n/a	n/a	n/a	5,000	5,000
Combined census/sample frames	19,082	885	2,853	5,344	5,000	5,000

affiliation, were not female, were not residing in the United States, or had left the group subsequent to the delivery of the gross set of presumptively unique member records.

This resulted in a gross group population that was then further reduced to eliminate those group members not contactable because the absence of a valid e-mail address. This left a net group population, which constitutes the "survey eligible" component of the membership. As such, the term *survey eligible* is not equivalent to each group's total membership at the time of the study, but rather is a subset of the overall membership.

For the three less populous groups, we conducted a census of the membership, that is, each survey-eligible member of the organization was invited to participate in the web-based survey. In the cases of the two more populous groups, MOPS and MomsRising, a random sample of five thousand of the survey-eligible members was drawn and these individuals were invited to participate. Thus, for these purposes we have both a "census frame" for the three less populous groups and "sample frame" for the two more populous groups. The outcomes of this process are set out in table A.1.

Internet Survey Instrument Summary, Respondent Contacting, Field Period, and Field Outcomes

Survey respondents were asked a battery of questions related to their involvement in their mothers' groups, their current arrangement of participating or not participating in the paid labor force, their attitudes toward workplace flexibility, and their preferences for how to encourage flexibility across American workplaces. The draft survey instrument was vetted by a panel of policy and survey experts.

Each respondent was given a unique nine-digit alphanumeric code; to facilitate order and tracking control, the first letter of that code reflected the respondent's group membership. This code was included in the subject line of each e-mail to each member so that bounce backs, rejections, and other undeliverables could be properly categorized for purposes of tracking contact rates. Again, to maintain order and tracking control over the survey sample, as well as to prevent overload on the survey's two hosting computer servers, each respondent contact was staggered by group over the course of the work week, from Monday through Friday as follows: NAMC, Mocha Moms, Mothers & More, MOPS, MomsRising.

Each respondent received an advance notice e-mail and, one week later, the initial e-mail invitation to complete the questionnaire. If the respondent did not take the survey, a week later she received a first follow-up-on-participation e-mail, a week after that a second follow-up-on-participation e-mail, and two weeks after that a third and final follow-up-on-participation e-mail. The survey was opened, and data collection commenced on Monday, April 20, 2009, continuing through Tuesday, June 2, 2009.

In addition to its stated purpose of announcing and priming the census populations and samples for the survey, the advance e-mail served as a final check on survey eligibility and e-mail address validity. Table A.2 shows, by group and overall, the counts of presumed eligible and contactable respondents who were revealed to be ineligible or noncontactable by way of advance e-mail bounce backs, as well as communications from potential respondents regarding their ineligibility. Moreover, when more than two of the four post-advance-e-mail communications were returned as undeliverable, that respondent was deemed noncontactable and, in turn, not "at risk" for being exposed to the survey. As such, the census and sample counts were, for the purposes of calculating response and refusal rates, reduced by these ineligibles and noncontactables. Still, the percentage of the original census and sample frames that remained eligible and contactable was notably high, at 94.5 percent overall, with the groups ranging from 89.7 percent to 97.4 percent. Table A.2 shows the distributions, overall and by group, of completed interviews, plenary nonresponses, and refusals.[1]

Internet Survey Response Analysis

Table A.3 presents an overview of the survey response overall and by group and includes calculations of response rates, refusal rates, and cooperation rates, along with the numerical counts necessary to derive those percentages. Here, the response rate is calculated in a manner consistent with the AAPOR3 response-rate calculation for the telephone survey, that is, we presume that the plenary nonresponses have an eligible-to-ineligible ratio (or a deliverable-to-nondeliverable ratio, or both) similar to the rest of the sample frame as shown in table A.2. This value, referred to as *e*, is used as a multiplier against the count of the plenary nonresponse to reduce that number to an empirically sustainable estimate of the eligible and contactable component of the plenary nonresponse categories.

In other words, since we do not have any information about the plenary nonresponse cases, and we do know, as a fact certain, that chunks of the presumed sample were ineligible, it is unreasonable to assume that every single one of those nonresponses is eligible. Thus, consistent with AAPOR formulas on point,[2] we reduced that category by a percentage equivalent to the proportion known to be eligible and contactable.

Internet Survey Performance Analysis, Margin of Sampling Error, and Weighting

Table A.4 presents a comparison of our pre-web-survey performance predications to our actual field performance. As noted in the main report, overall we achieved a response rate 4.3 points in excess of the predicted 15 percent, and each group, save MomsRising, achieved a response rate ranging from 1.0 to 11.4 points in excess of predictions.

Table A.4 also presents calculations for margins of sampling error. For all groups, the overall margin of sampling error was 1.7 percentage points at 95 percent confidence at the 45/55 margins. For MOPS and MomsRising, the two sampled groups, we are able to calculate true margins of sampling error. Those values report at 3.5 percentage points and 4.5 percentage points, respectively, at 95 percent confidence at the 45/55 margins. Because censuses were taken of the other three groups it is impossible to calculate a margin of sampling error; this is because, in a phrase, there was no sampling. However, we are able to generate an analog to the margin of sampling error that we have dubbed the "functional" margin of sampling error, by treating the number of completed interviews as a functional sample and conducting the standard sampling margin of error calculation on that basis. For these groups, those values ranged from 2.4 to 6.4 percentage points, within the common ranges expected. The fact that we have no information about whether

TABLE A.2.
Internet survey field outcomes

	All groups	NAMC	Mocha Moms	Mothers & More	MOPS	MomsRising
Final census/sample frames	19,082	885	2,853	5,344	5,000	5,000
Ineligible						
Not in/left group	29	3	9	4	3	10
Not mother	14	0	0	0	2	12
Duplicate	1	0	0	0	0	1
Not in United States	1	0	0	0	0	1
Noncontactable						
Advance e-mail bounce backs	814	29	59	150	100	476
50% or greater contact bounce backs	199	26	40	91	25	17
Eligible and contactable (%)	94.5	93.4	96.2	95.4	97.4	89.7
Presumed eligible contacted sample	18,024	827	2,745	5,099	4,870	4,483
Completed interview	3,327	182	620	1,302	762	461
Plenary nonresponse	14,637	644	2,119	3,781	4,100	3,993
Refused	60	1	6	16	8	29

TABLE A.3.
Internet survey response analysis

	All groups	NAMC	Mocha Moms	Mothers & More	MOPS	MomsRising
Eligible contacted census/sample	18,024	827	2,745	5,099	4,870	4,483
Completed interview	3,327	182	620	1,302	762	461
Refused	60	1	6	16	8	29
Plenary nonresponse	14,637	644	2,119	3,781	4,100	3,993
Estimate of eligibility of plenary nonresponses (%)	94.5	93.4	96.2	95.4	97.4	89.7
e (estimated eligibility multiplier)	0.945	0.934	0.962	0.954	0.974	0.897
Response rate (%)	19.3	23.2	23.3	26.4	16.0	11.3
Refusal rate (%)	0.3	0.1	0.2	0.3	0.2	0.7
Cooperation rate (known eligible contacts only) (%)	98.2	99.5	99.0	98.8	99.0	94.1

TABLE A.4.
Internet survey target-to-performance analysis and margin of sampling error calculations[a]

	All groups	NAMC	Mocha Moms	Mothers & More	MOPS	MomsRising
Net group population	262,452	885	2,853	5,344	84,584	168,786
Combined census/sample frames	19,082	885	2,853	5,344	5,000	5,000
Predicted response rate (%)	15.0	15.0	15.0	15.0	15.0	15.0
Actual response rate (%)	19.3	23.2	23.3	26.4	16.0	11.3
Response rate, predicted-to-actual deviation (%)	+4.3	+8.2	+8.3	+11.4	+1.0	−3.7
Predicted count of completed interviews	2,862	133	428	802	750	750
Actual count of completed interviews	3,327	182	620	1,302	762	461
Completed interviews, predicted-to-actual deviation	+465	+49	+192	+500	+12	−289
Margin of sampling error to net group population (percentage points)	1.7	n/a	n/a	n/a	3.5	4.5
Functional margin of sampling error to net group population (percentage points)	n/a	6.4	3.5	2.4	n/a	n/a

[a] 95% confidence, 45/55 margins.

the members who fell into plenary nonresponse category were ever "at risk of exposure" to the survey provides a presumed theoretical justification for treating the category of completed interviews as a sample of the whole population.

Last, because the groups do not collect sufficient demographic population parameters on their memberships (and, as such, have no population targets for the groups), we were unable to weight these data to coax the completed sample demography to better approximate the group census and sample frame demography. However, given the composition of these groups in combination with the eligibility requirements for qualifying for the survey, logic and common sense compel that no weighting is necessary. The groups are largely homogeneous populations; as such, there is no theoretical or empirical basis on which to argue that poststratification adjustments are necessary in this instance.

Nationwide Random Sample Telephone Survey

The following is an executive summary of all significant parameters for the nationwide random sample telephone survey:

Completed interviews	800
Respondents	Mothers (female guardians) of children under 18
Incidence rate	23.0 percent (estimated) 11.7 percent (screening)
AAPOR3 response rate	46.4 percent
AAPOR3 cooperation rate	67.2 percent
Margin of sampling error	3.4 percentage points at 95 percent confidence at the 45 percent / 55 percent margins
Pretest	Monday, April 6, 2009 (n = 10)
Field period	Tuesday, April 14, through Tuesday, June 2, 2009
Mean interview duration	17.2 minutes
Sampling approach	National RDD sample, continental United States

Call design   Six-call design; one refusal
                               conversion on all soft refusals
Weighting schema   ((Age x sex) x region)

The Telephone Survey Instrument, Sampling Protocol, and Field
Procedures

Because the key purpose of the telephone survey was to provide national
control and comparison data for the web survey of the five groups' members, the telephone questionnaire was constructed primarily as a subset
of the web survey inquiries. While some of the web survey questions
were not included on the telephone survey, all the telephone survey
questions except the respondent-qualification screening and consent
questions were reflected on the web survey. Qualification screens were
put in place to assure that the respondent was at least eighteen years of
age and consented to the survey; that there was at least one child, age
seventeen or under, living in the subject household; that the respondent
was the mother, stepmother, or guardian of at least one such child; and
that the respondent was not a member of any one of the five mothers'
groups participating in the web survey.

Assuming that the respondent qualified for survey participation,
the interviewer proceeded with the telephone survey instrument,
probing the follow areas of inquiry: (1) work/employment for pay;
(2) characteristics of employer; (3) impact of parenting responsibilities
on relationship with employer; (4) conditions of employment, that is,
workplace flexibility options; (5) attitudes, interests, and preferences
with regard to government intervention on the issue of workplace
flexibility options; and (6) demography and related statistical control
variables.

After pretesting ten interviews on Monday, April 6, 2009, the ran-
dom-digit-dial telephone survey was fielded from Tuesday, April 14
through Tuesday, June 2, 2009. Calling continued daily throughout on
a six-call design (with one refusal conversion effort on all soft refusals), targeting and achieving eight hundred completed interviews. The
survey was administered in both English and Spanish; 737 interviews
(92.1%) were conducted in English and 63 interviews (7.9%) were conducted in Spanish.

Telephone Survey Response Analysis and Sampling Error

We deployed the AAPOR3 method of response-rate calculation for the nationwide random telephone survey; that formula yielded a 46.4 percent survey response rate. Similarly, the AAPOR COOP3 cooperation rate was calculated at 67.2. To give these metrics some meaning, in common terms a 46 percent response rate indicates that by random selection we were able to complete an interview with a resident in just under one out of every two households that qualified for participation in the survey. Similarly, a 67 percent cooperation rate means that we were able to randomly interview persons in over two out of every three qualified households that we were able to contact.

Sampling error, which is the probable difference in response, at a fixed degree of statistical confidence, between interviewing everyone in a given population and a sample drawn from that population, is inversely proportional to sample size; in other words, sampling error decreases as the effective sample size increases, largely without regard for the size of the population under study provided that the population is greater than ten thousand. In this case, the April 2009 Current Population Survey data estimates a population of 36,308,416 of "females age 18 and older with their own children under the age of 18," yielding a 3.4 percentage point margin of error for eight hundred completed interviews.[3]

Sampling error increases as the effective sample size is reduced. This fact must be kept in mind when comparing the responses of different groups *within* the sample, for example, mothers who work for pay outside the home compared with stay-at-home mothers, or younger compared with older respondents. While it is perfectly acceptable in survey research to report the overall margin of sampling error, it technically should be calculated based on bivariate responses to each separate question in the survey for each subgroup of interest.[4]

Telephone Survey Weighting

Population targets for age, race-ethnicity, and geographic region were drawn from the April 2009 Current Population Survey data for "adult females and households with own children under 18." Because of the absence of reliable distribution data on other household structure

TABLE A.5.
Telephone survey post-stratification weighting population targets

	Number of Persons	Percentage Breakdown
RACE		
Non-Hispanic white	21, 936, 720	60.42
Non-Hispanic black	4,828,211	13.30
Hispanic	6,886,583	18.97
Other	2,656,902	7.32
Total	36,308,416	100.00
AGE		
18–34	13,946,526	38.41
35–44	14,242,979	39.23
45–54	7,178,594	19.77
55+	940,318	2.59
Total	36,308,417	100.00
REGION		
Northeast	6,237,548	17.18
Midwest (formerly North Central)	7,983,661	21.99
South	13,382,443	36.86
West	8,704,764	23.97
Total	36,308,416	100.00

scenarios, such as adopted or foster children, as well as cases where the household female was not the primary caregiver, we were constrained to use the "own children" heuristic. The distribution of population targets is shown in table A.5.

Under an ((age x race-ethnicity) x geography) schema, age target groupings were taken as 18–34, 35–44, 45–54, and 55+; race was determined as "non-Hispanic white," "non-Hispanic black," "Hispanic," and "other"; and geography was based on four subnational regions: Northeast, Midwest, South, and West. In all cases, missing cells were given a neutral value of 1.0. The weight variable has a mean value of 1.0, a standard deviation of 0.4442, and a range from 0.3275 to 2.1482.

Notes

1. American Mothers, American Troubles

1. Much of this discussion is based on President's Obama's recollections in Barack Obama, *The Audacity of Hope: Thoughts on Reclaiming the American Dream* (New York: Crown, 2006).

2. This categorization scheme was developed by Workplace Flexibility 2010, an organization located at Georgetown University Law Center and funded by the Alfred P. Sloan Foundation's Workplace, Work Force, and Working Families Program.

3. Ellen Galinsky, James T. Bond, and E. Jeffrey Hill, *When Work Works: A Status Report on Workplace Flexibility* (New York: Work and Families Institute, 2004); WFD, *The New Career Paradigm: Flexibility Briefing* (Newton, MA: WFD Consulting, 2007).

4. Joseph G. Grzywacz, Dawn S. Carlson, and Sandee Shulkin, "Schedule Flexibility and Stress: Linking Formal Flexible Arrangements and Perceived Flexibility to Employee Health," *Community, Work and Family* 11, no. 2 (2008): 199–214; Amy L. Richman, Janet T. Civian, Laurie L. Shannon, E. Jeffrey Hill, and Robert T. Brennan, "The Relationship of Perceived Flexibility, Supportive Work-Life Policies, and Use of Formal Flexible Arrangements and Occasional Flexibility to Employee Engagement and Expected Retention," *Community, Work and Family* 11, no. 2 (2008): 183–97; Patrick R. Casey and Joseph G. Grzywacz, "Employee Health and Well-Being: The Role of Flexibility and Work-Family Balance," *Psychologist-Manager Journal* 11, no. 1 (2008): 31–47.

5. Lillian T. Eby, Wendy J. Casper, Angie Lockwood, Chris Bordeaux, and Andi Brinley, "Work and Family Research in IO/OB: Content Analysis and Review of the Literature (1980–2002)," *Journal of Vocational Behavior* 61, no. 1 (2005): 92–108; Stella E. Anderson, Betty S. Coffey, and Robin T. Byerly, "Formal Organizational Initiatives and Informal Workplace Practices: Links to Work-Family Conflict and Job-Related Outcomes," *Journal of Management* 28, no. 6 (2002): 787–810.

6. Janet C. Gornick and Marcia K. Meyers, *Families That Work: Policies for Reconciling Parenthood and Employment* (New York City: Russell Sage Foundation, 2003).

7. Sandra L. Hofferth and Sally C. Curtin, "Parental Leave Statutes and Maternal Return to Work after Childbirth in the United States," *Work and Occupations* 33, no. 1 (2006): 73–105.

8. Sylvia Ann Hewlett, *Off-Ramps and On-Ramps: Keeping Talented Women on the Road to Success* (Boston: Harvard Business School Press, 2007); Sylvia Ann Hewlett and Carolyn Buck Luce, "Off-Ramps and On-Ramps," *Harvard Business Review* 83, no. 3 (2005): 43–54; Pamela Stone, *Opting Out? Why Women Really Quit Careers and Head Home* (Berkeley: University of California Press, 2007).

9. Shoba V. Arun, Thankom G. Arun, and Vani K. Borooah, "The Effect of Career Breaks on the Working Lives of Women," *Feminist Economics* 10, no. 3 (2004): 65–84; Lori L. Reid, "Occupational Segregation, Human Capital, and Motherhood: Black Women's Higher Exit Rates from Full-Time Employment," *Gender and Society* 16, no. 10 (2002): 728–47.

10. Joan Williams, *Unbending Gender: Why Family and Work Conflict and What to Do about It* (New York: Oxford University Press, 2000).

11. Hewlett, *Off-Ramps and On-Ramps*; Charles Baum, "The Effects of Maternity Leave Legislation on Mother's Labor Supply after Childbirth," *Southern Economic Journal* 69, no. 4 (2003): 772–99.

12. Dan R. Dalton and Debra J. Mesch, "The Impact of Flexible Scheduling on Employee Attendance and Turnover," *Administrative Science Quarterly* 35, no. 2 (1990): 370–87; Georges Dionne and Benoit Dostie, "New Evidence on the Determinants of Absenteeism Using Linked Employer-Employee Data," *Industrial and Labor Relations Review* 61, no. 1 (2007): 108–20.

13. Kathleen E. Christensen and Graham L. Staines, "Flextime: A Viable Solution to Work/Family Conflict," *Journal of Family Issues* 11, no. 4 (1990): 455–76; Barbara Gault and Vicky Lovell, "The Costs and Benefits of Policies to Advance Work/Life Integration," *American Behavioral Scientist* 49, no. 9 (2006): 1152–62.

14. Williams, *Unbending Gender*.

15. Ellen Galinsky, James T. Bond, and Kelly Sakai, *2008 National Study of Employers* (New York: Families and Work Institute, 2008).

16. Executive Office of the President, Council of Economic Advisers, *Work-Life Balance and the Economics of Workplace Flexibility* (Washington, DC: Executive Office of the President, Council of Economic Advisers, 2010).

17. Corporate Voices for Working Families, *Workplace Flexibility for Lower Wage Workers* (Waltham, MA: WFD Consulting, 2006).

18. Jeffrey E. Hill, Jenet I. Jacob, Laurie L. Shannon, Robert T. Brennan, Victoria L. Blanchard, and Giuseppe Martinengo, "Exploring the Relationship of Workplace Flexibility, Gender, and Life Stage to Family-to-Work Conflict, and Stress and Burnout," *Community, Work, and Family* 11, no. 2 (2008): 165–81.

19. Williams, *Unbending Gender.*

20. Susan C. Eaton, "If You Can Use Them: Flexibility Policies, Organizational Commitment, and Perceived Performance," *Industrial Relations* 42, no. 2 (2003): 145–67.

21. BLS, American Time Use Survey, table A-6, 2011, http://www.bls.gov/tus/tables/a6_0509.pdf.

22. Kristin A. Goss and Michael T. Heaney, "Organizing Women as Women: Hybridity and Grassroots Collective Action in the 21st Century," *Perspectives on Politics* 8, no. 1 (2010): 27–52.

23. This discussion is meant to include all groups with a primary focus on organizations dealing with mothers' issues. Groups also had to eventually be located in more than one state for inclusion and to have had more than twenty-five thousand members at least once during their history.

24. Theda Skocpol, *Protecting Soldiers and Mothers: The Political Origins of Social Policy in the United States* (Cambridge: Harvard University Press, 1992).

25. General Federation of Women's Clubs, "History and Mission," General Federation of Women's Clubs, 2010, http://www.gfwc.org/gfwc/history_and_mission.asp?snid=1799682275.

26. Deborah Gray White, *Too Heavy a Load: Black Women in Defense of Themselves, 1894–1994* (New York: W. W. Norton, 1999).

27. Skocpol, *Protecting Soldiers and Mothers.*

28. Administration for Children and Families, U.S. Department of Health and Human Services, http://www.acf.hhs.gov/.

29. Planned Parenthood Federation of America, "History and Successes," http://www.plannedparenthood.org/about-us/who-we-are/history-and-successes.htm.

30. Jo Freeman, "On the Origins of Social Movements," in *Waves of Protest: Social Movements since the Sixties,* ed. J. Freeman and V. Johnson (Lanham, MD: Rowman and Littlefield, 1999).

31. Lawrence Neil Bailis, *Bread or Justice: Grassroots Organizing in the Welfare Rights Movement* (Lexington, MA: Lexington Books, 1974).

32. Lynn Y. Weiner, "Reconstructing Motherhood: The La Leche League in Postwar America," *Journal of American History* 80, no. 4 (1994): 1357–81.

33. Laurie Davies, *25 Years of Saving Lives*, Mothers Against Drunk Driving, http://www.madd.org/about-us/history/madd25thhistory.pdf.

34. Craig Reinarman, "Social Construction of an Alcohol Problem: The Case of Mothers Against Drunk Drivers and Social Control in the 1980s," *Theory and Society* 17, no. 1 (1988): 91–120.

35. Brady Campaign to Prevent Gun Violence, "Million Mom March–Brady Campaign to Prevent Gun Violence," http://www.bradycampaign.org/about/history.

36. Other mothers' groups certainly exist, especially at the local level. But these tend to be small and unstructured, which make them difficult to study. See the appendix for more information on these issues.

37. Andrea O'Reilly, "Maternal Activism as Matricentric Feminism: The History, Ideological Frameworks, Political Strategies, and Activist Practices of the 21st Century Motherhood Movement," in *The 21st Century Motherhood Movement: Mothers Speak Out on Why We Need to Change the World and How to Do It*, ed. Andrea O'Reilly (Bradford, ON: Demeter, 2011).

38. BLS, *Women in the Labor Force: A Databook* (Washington, DC: Department of Labor, 2011).

39. Sharon Hays, *The Cultural Contradictions of Motherhood* (New Haven: Yale University Press, 1996); Angela Hattery, *Women, Work, and Family: Balancing and Weaving* (Thousand Oaks, CA: Sage, 2001).

40. Kathleen Gerson, *Hard Choices: How Women Decide about Work, Career, and Motherhood* (Berkeley and Los Angeles: University of California Press, 1985).

41. Note that all these membership numbers are from 2009, when the majority of the study components were conducted.

42. Carla M. Eastis, "Organizing Ideologies of Motherhood" (PhD diss., Yale University, 2004).

43. To qualify as a theme in the interview responses sections, at least 10 percent, or thirteen, of the respondents had to identify it as such.

44. Terry Arendell, "Conceiving and Investigating Motherhood: The Decade's Scholarship," *Journal of Marriage and the Family* 62, no. 4 (2000): 1192–207.

45. Patricia A. Roos, Mary K. Trigg, and Mary S. Hartman, "Changing Families/Changing Communities: Work, Family, and Community in Transition," *Community, Work, and Family* 9, no. 2 (2006): 197–224.

2. Power in Numbers

1. Much of this information comes from discussions in 2008–9 with Karen Parks, director of Strategic Relations for MOPS, and Naomi Michie, a founding member of MOPS, as well as the MOPS website, www.mops.org.

2. Much of this information comes from discussions in 2008–9 with Mocha Moms co-founder and president emerita Cheli English-Figaro and www.mocha moms.org.

3. Much of this history is based on discussions in 2008–9 with organizational founder Joanne Brundage and www.mothersandmore.org.

4. See Carla M. Eastis, "Organizing Ideologies of Motherhood" (PhD diss., Yale University, 2004), 67.

5. Linda Chion-Kenney, "Another Way to Have It All," *Washington Post*, May 31, 1988.

6. Arlene Rossen Cardozo, *Sequencing* (New York: Collier, 1986).

7. Christine Davidson, *Staying Home Instead: How to Quit the Working-Mom Rat Race and Survive Financially* (Lexington, MA: Lexington Books, 1986); Deborah Fallows, *A Mother's Work* (Boston: Houghton Mifflin, 1985).

8. Eastis, "Organizing Ideologies of Motherhood."

9. Much of this section comes from discussions in 2008–9 with NAMC president Linda Juergens and www.motherscenter.org.

10. Ann Crittenden, *The Price of Motherhood* (New York: Henry Holt, 2001).

11. Much of this information comes from discussions in 2008–9 with MomsRising founder Joan Blades and www.momsrising.org.

12. Kristin Rowe-Finkbeiner, *The F-Word: Feminism in Jeopardy* (Emeryville, CA: Seal Press, 2004).

13. Joan Blades and Kristin Rowe-Finkbeiner, *The Motherhood Manifesto: What America's Moms Want—and What to Do about It* (New York: Nation Books, 2006).

3. Why Join?

1. Recall that MomsRising, however, does not have chapters.

2. For examples of how mothers have come together in this inward way, offering each other skills and emotional support, see John W. Gibson and Lorraine Gutierrez, "A Service Program for Safe-Home Children," *Families in Society* 72, no. 9 (1991): 554–62; Kris Kissman and Ophelia A. Torres, "Incarcerated Mothers: Mutual Support Groups Aimed at Reducing Substance Abuse Relapse and Recidivism," *Contemporary Family Therapy: An International Journal* 26, no. 2 (2004): 217–28; Rae J. Memmott and Laurie A. Young, "An Encounter with Homeless Mothers and Children: Gaining an Awareness," *Issues in Mental Health Nursing* 14, no. 4 (1993): 357–65; Denise Côté-Arsenault and Marsha Mason Freije, "Support Groups Helping Women through Pregnancies after Loss," *Western Journal of Nursing Research* 26, no. 6 (2004): 650–70. For examples of how mothers have come together to generate support in this inward way as they relate to new familial roles, see Jane D. Bock, "Doing the

Right Thing? Single Mothers by Choice and the Struggle for Legitimacy," *Gender and Society* 14, no. 1 (2000): 62–86; Allison Christian, "Contesting the Myth of the 'Wicked Stepmother': Narrative Analysis of an Online Stepfamily Support Group," *Western Journal of Communication* 69, no. 1 (2005): 27–47.

3. John Mark Hansen, *Gaining Access: Congress and the Farm Lobby, 1919–1981* (Chicago: University of Chicago Press, 1991); Frances E. Lee, "Interests, Constituencies, and Policy Making," in *The Legislative Branch*, ed. P. J. Quirk and S. A. Binder (New York: Oxford University Press, 2005).

4. Frank R. Baumgartner and Beth L. Leech, *Basic Interests: The Importance of Groups in Politics and in Political Science* (Princeton: Princeton University Press, 1998).

5. Christopher B. Wlezien and Malcolm L. Goggin, "The Courts, Interest Groups, and Public Opinion about Abortion " *Political Behavior* 15, no. 4 (1993): 381–405; Lee, "Interests, Constituencies, and Policy Making."

6. Darrell M. West and Richard Francis, "Electronic Advocacy: Interest Groups and Public Policymaking," *PS: Political Science and Politics* 29, no. 1 (1996): 25–29.

7. Anne Hildreth, "The Importance of Purposes in 'Purposive' Groups: Incentives and Participation in the Sanctuary Movement," *American Journal of Political Science* 38, no. 2 (1994): 447–63.

8. Thomas L. Gais and Jack L. Walker, "Pathways to Influence in American Politics," in *Mobilizing Interest Groups in America*, ed. J. L. Walker (Ann Arbor: University of Michigan Press, 1991).

4. Barriers to Organizing for Workplace Flexibility

1. Viviana Zelizer, *Pricing the Priceless Child: The Changing Social Value of Children* (Princeton: Princeton University Press, 1994).

2. Sharon Hays, *The Cultural Contradictions of Motherhood* (New Haven: Yale University Press, 1996); Angela Hattery, *Women, Work, and Family: Balancing and Weaving* (Thousand Oaks, CA: Sage, 2001); Anita I. Garey, "Constructing Motherhood on the Night Shift: "Working Mothers" as Stay-at Home Moms," *Qualitative Sociology* 18, no. 4 (1995): 414–37.

3. Annette Lareau, *Unequal Childhoods: Class, Race, and Family Life* (Berkeley and Los Angeles: University of California Press, 2003).

4. Joan Williams, *Unbending Gender: Why Family and Work Conflict and What to Do about It* (New York: Oxford University Press, 2000); Joan Williams, *Reshaping the Work-Family Debate: Why Men and Class Matter* (Cambridge: Harvard University Press, 2010).

5. Ann Crittenden, *The Price of Motherhood* (New York: Henry Holt, 2001); Mary Blair-Loy, *Competing Devotions: Career and Family among Women Executives* (Cambridge: Harvard University Press, 2003).

6. Deirdre D. Johnston and Debra H. Swanson, "Moms Hating Moms: The Internalization of Mother War Rhetoric," *Sex Roles* 51, nos. 9/10 (2004): 497–508.

7. Miriam Peskowitz, *The Truth behind the Mommy Wars: Who Decides What Makes a Good Mother?* (Emeryville, CA: Seal Press, 2005).

8. Johnston and Swanson, "Moms Hating Moms"; Toni Schindler Zimmerman, Jennifer T. Aberle, Jennifer L. Krafchick, and Ashley M. Harvey, "Deconstructing the 'Mommy Wars': The Battle over the Best Mom," *Journal of Feminist Family Therapy* 20, no. 3 (2008): 203–19.

9. Deirdre D. Johnston and Debra H. Swanson, "Constructing the 'Good Mother': The Internalization of Mother War Rhetoric," *Sex Roles* 54, nos. 7/8 (2006): 509–19; Debra H. Swanson and Deirdre D. Johnston, "Mothering in the Ivy Tower: Interviews with Academic Mothers," *Journal of the Association for Research on Mothering* 5, no. 2 (2003): 63–75; Blair-Loy, *Competing Devotions*.

10. Pamela Stone, *Opting Out? Why Women Really Quit Careers and Head Home* (Berkeley and Los Angeles: University of California Press, 2007); Sylvia Ann Hewlett, *Off-Ramps and On-Ramps: Keeping Talented Women on the Road to Success* (Boston: Harvard Business School Press, 2007).

11. Blair-Loy, *Competing Devotions*; Noam Shpancer, Katherine M. Melick, Pamela S. Sayre, and Aria T. Spivey, "Quality of Care Attributions to Employed versus Stay-at-Home Mothers," *Early Child Development and Care* 176, no. 2 (2006): 183–93; Stacy E. Rubin and H. Ray Wooten, "Highly Educated Stay-at-Home Mothers: A Study of Commitment and Conflict," *Family Journal* 15, no. 4 (2007): 336–45; Janet Zollinger Giele, "Homemaker or Career Woman: Life Course Factors and Racial Influences among Middle Class Americans," *Journal of Comparative Family Studies* 39, no. 3 (2008): 393–411.

12. Johnston and Swanson, "Moms Hating Moms."

13. Shpancer, Melick, Sayre, and Spivey, "Quality of Care Attributions"; Darlene C. DeFour and Tamara Mose Brown, "Attitudes towards Maternal Roles the Effects on Life Satisfaction: Black, Hispanic, and White Models," *Journal of African American Studies* 10, no. 3 (2006): 3–18.

14. Peskowitz, *The Truth behind the Mommy Wars*; Mary Douglas Vavrus, "Opting Out Moms in the News: Selling New Traditionalism in the New Millennium," *Feminist Media Studies* 7, no. 1 (2007): 47–63.

5. Workplace Flexibility Options

1. Laura M. Hecht, "Role Conflict and Role Overload: Different Concepts, Different Consequences," *Sociological Inquiry* 71, no. 1 (2001): 111–21; Carol J. Erdwins, Louis C. Buffardi, Wendy J. Casper, and Alison S. O'Brien, "The Relationship of Women's Role Strain to Social Support, Role Satisfaction, and Self-Efficacy," *Family Relations* 50, no. 3 (2001): 230–38; Esther R. Greenglass, Kaye-Lee Pantony, and Ronald J. Burke, "A Gender-Role Perspective on Role

Conflict, Work Stress, and Social Support," *Journal of Social Behavior and Personality* 3, no. 4 (1988): 317–28.

2. Hecht, "Role Conflict and Role Overload"; Faye J. Crosby, *Juggling* (New York: Free Press, 1991).

3. An opposing point of view, however, argues that individuals benefit greatly from holding multiple roles with respect to a positive self-identity, purpose, and meaning in life. See Peggy A. Thoits, "Personal Agency in the Accumulation of Multiple Role-Identities," in *Advances in Identity Theory and Research*, ed. P. J. Burke, T. J. Owens, R. Serpe and P. A. Thoits (New York: Kluwer Academic/Plenum, 2003). In addition, while perhaps experiencing role conflict and role overload, employed mothers generally have higher rates of mental health than stay-at-home mothers. See Rebekah Levine Coley, Brenda J. Lohman, Elizabeth Votruba-Drzal, Laura D. Pittman, and P. Lindsay Chase-Lansdale, "Maternal Functioning, Time, and Money: The World of Work and Welfare," *Children and Youth Services* 29, no. 6 (2007): 721–41. See also Cheryl Buehler and Marion O'Brien, "Mothers' Part-Time Employment: Associations with Mother and Family Well-Being," *Journal of Family Psychology* 25, no. 6 (2011): 895–906.

4. Recall that in order to count as a theme in this book, at least 10 percent, or thirteen respondents, must identify it as such. The 10 percent rule applies here as well. However, it is applied in each case separately to mothers working for pay (numbering seventy-five in total) and stay-at-home moms (numbering fifty in total) for each category of responses.

6. Are We in a Movement Now? Can We Get There?

1. Francesca Polletta and James M. Jasper, "Collective Identity and Social Movements," *Annual Review of Sociology* 27 (2001): 283–305; Ed Collom and Douglas E. Mitchell, "Home Schooling as a Social Movement: Identifying the Determinants of Homeschoolers' Perceptions," *Sociological Spectrum* 25, no. 3 (2005): 273–305.

2. Marc Dixon and Vincent J. Roscigno, "Status, Networks, and Social Movement Participation: The Case of Striking Workers," *American Journal of Sociology* 108, no. 6 (2003): 1292–1327; Bert Klandermans, *The Social Psychology of Protest* (Oxford, UK: Blackwell, 1997); Florence Passy and Marco Giugni, "Social Networks and Individual Perceptions: Explaining Differential Participation in Social Movements," *Sociological Forum* 16, no. 1 (2001): 123–53.

3. Hank Johnston, Enrique Larana, and Joseph R. Gusfield, "Identities, Grievances, and New Social Movements," in *New Social Movements: From Ideology to Identity*, ed. E. Larana, H. Johnston, and J. R. Gusfield (Philadelphia: Temple University Press, 1994); Verta Taylor, "Gender and Social Movements: Gender Processes in Women's Self-Help Movements," *Gender and Society* 13, no. 1

(1999): 8–33; Joshua Gamson, "Messages of Exclusion: Gender, Movements, and Symbolic Boundaries," *Gender and Society* 11, no. 2 (1997): 178–99; George T. Crane, "Collective Identity, Symbolic Mobilization, and Student Protest in Nanjing, China, 1988–1989," *Comparative Politics* 26, no. 4 (1994): 395–413.

4. Sheldon Stryker, "Identity Competition: Key to Differential Social Movement Participation," in *Self, Identity, and Social Movements*, ed. S. Stryker, T. J. Owens and R. W. White (Minneapolis: University of Minnesota Press, 2000).

5. Ziad Munson, *The Making of Pro-life Activists: How Social Movement Mobilization Works* (Chicago: University of Chicago Press, 2009).

6. Janet C. Gornick and Marcia K. Meyers, *Families That Work: Policies for Reconciling Parenthood and Employment* (New York City: Russell Sage Foundation, 2003).

7. Mothers Need Leadership Too

1. Michelle Obama, "Michelle Obama's Remarks at Workplace Flexibility Conference," March 31, 2010, *Washington Post*, http://www.washingtonpost.com/wp-dyn/content/article/2010/03/31/AR2010033103642.html.

2. Wendell Joice, *The Evolution of Telework in the Federal Government* (Washington, DC: U.S. General Services Administration, 2000).

3. Workplace Flexibility 2010, *Public Policy Platform on Flexible Work Arrangements* (Washington, DC: Workplace Flexibility 2010: Georgetown Law, n.d.), http://workplaceflexibility2010.org/images/uploads/reports/report_1.pdf.

4. *Northern Virginia Technology Council*, "Governor McDonnell Signs NVTC-Backed Telework Tax Credit and Transportation Investment Legislation," http://www.nvtc.org/news/getnewscontent.php?code=314 (accessed September 24, 2012).

5. Georgia Department of Revenue, 2010 Tax Credits Description; https://etax.dor.ga.gov/inctax/taxcredits/2010_Tax_Credit_Summaries.pdf (accessed September 25, 2012).

6. Workplace Flexibility 2010, *The United Kingdom Flexible Working Act* (Washington, DC: Workplace Flexibility 2010: Georgetown Law, n.d.). http://workplaceflexibility2010.org/index.php/laws_impacting_flexibility/UK_FWA.

7. Workplace Flexibility 2010, *Public Policy Platform on Flexible Work Arrangements* (Washington, DC: Workplace Flexibility 2010: Georgetown Law, n.d.), http://workplaceflexibility2010.org/images/uploads/reports/report_1.pdf.

8. Ellen Ernst Kossek, "Work and Family in America: Growing Tensions between Employment Policy and a Transformed Workforce; a Thirty Year Perspective," in *America at Work: Choices and Challenges*, ed. E. E. Lawler and J. O'Toole (New York: Palgrave Macmillan, 2006).

9. Costas Panagopoulos and Peter L. Francia, "The Polls: Trends-Labor Unions in the United States," *Public Opinion Quarterly* 72, no. 1 (2008): 134–59.

10. Steven L. Nock and Paul W. Kingston, "Time with Children: The Impact of Couples' Work-Time Commitments," *Social Forces* 67, no. 1 (1988): 59–85; Carol S. Wharton, "Finding Time for the "Second Shift": The Impact of Flexible Work Schedules on Women's Double Days," *Gender and Society* 8, no. 2 (1994): 189–205.

11. Hilary Silver, "Homework and Domestic Work," *Sociological Forum* 18, no. 2 (1993): 181–204; Hilary Silver and Frances Goldscheider, "Flexible Work and Housework: Work and Family Constraints on Women's Domestic Labor," *Social Forces* 72, no. 4 (1994): 1103–19; Mary C. Noonan, Sarah Beth Estes, and Jennifer L. Glass, "Do Workplace Flexibility Policies Influence Time Spent in Domestic Labor?," *Journal of Family Issues* 28, no. 2 (2007): 263–88.

12. Michelle J. Budig and Melissa J. Hodges, "Differences in Disadvantage: Variation in the Motherhood Penalty across White Women's Earnings Distribution," *American Sociological Review* 75, no. 5 (2010): 705–28; Jane Waldfogel, "The Effects of Children on Women's Wages," *American Sociological Review* 62, no. 2 (1997): 209–17; Kathleen Fuegen, Monica Biernat, Elizabeth Haines, and Kay Deaux, "Mothers and Fathers in the Workplace: How Gender and Parental Status Influence Judgments of Job-Related Competence," *Journal of Social Issues* 60, no. 4 (2004): 737–54; Sara J. Corse, "Pregnant Managers and Their Subordinates: The Effects of Gender Expectations on Hierarchical Relationships," *Journal of Applied Behavioral Science* 26, no. 1 (1990): 25–28; Jane A. Halpert, Midge L. Wilson, and Julia L. Hickman, "Pregnancy as a Source of Bias in Performance Appraisals," *Journal of Organizational Behavior* 14, no. 7 (1993): 649–63.

13. Shelley J. Correll, Stephen Benard, and In Paik, "Getting a Job: Is There a Motherhood Penalty?," *American Journal of Sociology* 112, no. 5 (2007): 1297–1338; Amy J. C. Cuddy, Susan Fiske, and Peter Glick, "When Professionals Become Mothers, Warmth Doesn't Cut the Ice," *Journal of Social Issues* 60, no. 4 (2004): 701–18; Claire Etaugh and Denise Folger, "Perceptions of Parents Whose Work and Parenting Behaviors Deviate from Role Expectations," *Sex Roles* 39, nos. 3/4 (1998): 215–23; Stephen Benard and Shelley J. Correll, "Normative Discrimination and the Motherhood Penalty," *Gender and Society* 24, no. 5 (2010): 616–46.

14. Kathleen Gerson, *The Unfinished Revolution: How a New Generation Is Reshaping Family, Work, and Gender in America* (New York: Oxford University Press, 2010); Sara Ruddick, *Maternal Thinking: Toward a Politics of Peace* (Boston: Beacon Press, 1989).

15. Susan J. Lambert, " 'Opting In" to Full Labor Force Participation in Hourly Jobs," in *Women Who Opt Out: The Debate over Working Mothers and Work-Family Balance*, ed. B. D. Jones (New York: New York University Press, 2012).

16. Maureen Perry-Jenkins, "The Challenges to and Consequences of 'Opting Out' for Low-Wage, New Mothers," in *Women Who Opt Out: The Debate over Working Mothers and Work-Family Balance*, ed. B. D. Jones (New York: New York University Press, 2012).

17. Bob Edwards and John D. McCarthy, "Strategy Matters: The Contingent Value of Social Capital in the Survival of Local Social Movement Organizations," *Social Forces* 83, no. 2 (2004): 621–51; Marieke Van Willigen and Verta Taylor, "Women's Self-Help and the Reconstruction of Gender: The Postpartum Support and Breast Cancer Movements," *Mobilization* 1, no. 2 (1996): 123–42.

18. William Gamson, *Talking Politics* (New York: Cambridge University Press, 1992).

19. Michael L. Schwalbe and Douglas Mason-Schrock, "Identity Work as Group Process," *Advances in Group Processes* 13 (1996): 113–47; David A. Snow and Leon Anderson, "Identity Work among the Homeless: The Verbal Construction and Avowal of Personal Identities," *American Journal of Sociology* 92 (1987): 1336–71; David A. Snow and Doug McAdam, "Identity Work Processes in the Context of Social Movements: Clarifying the Identity/Movement Nexus," in *Self, Identity, and Social Movements*, ed. S. Stryker, T. J. Owens, and R. White (Minneapolis: University of Minnesota Press, 2000); Rachel L. Einwohner, "Identity Work and Collective Action in a Repressive Context: Jewish Resistance on the "Aryan Side" of the Warsaw Ghetto," *Social Problems* 53, no. 1 (2006): 38–56.

20. Jocelyn Elise Crowley, "On the Cusp of a Movement: Identity Work and Social Movement Identification Processes within Fathers' Rights Groups," *Sociological Spectrum* 28, no. 6 (2008): 705–24.

21. Rachel L. Einwohner, Jo Reger, and Daniel Myers, "Introduction: Identity Work, Sameness, and Difference in Movements," in *Identity Work in Social Movements*, ed. J. Reger, D. Myers and R. L. Einwohner (Minneapolis: University of Minnesota Press, 2008).

22. K. Jill Kiecolt, "Self-Change in Social Movements," in *Self, Identity, and Social Movements*, ed. S. Stryker, T. J. Owens and R. White (Minneapolis: University of Minnesota Press, 2000); Paul Lichterman, "Talking Identity in the Public Sphere: Broad Visions and Small Spaces in Sexual Identity Politics," *Theory and Society* 28, no. 1 (1999): 101–41; Robert Wuthnow, *Sharing the Journey: Support Groups and America's New Quest for Community* (New York: Free Press, 1994).

23. Scott A. Hunt and Robert D. Benford, "Identity Talk in the Peace and Justice Movement," *Journal of Contemporary Ethnography* 22, no. 4 (1994): 488–517; Edward J. Walsh, "Resource Mobilization and Citizen Protest in Communities around Three Mile Island," *Social Problems* 29, no. 1 (1981): 1–21.

24. Kiecolt, "Self-Change in Social Movements."

Appendix

1. By *plenary nonresponse* we mean that there was absolutely no information whatsoever gleaned from or about the respondent from the advance e-mail or any of the four main e-mail communications. This includes the absence of a bounce back, "over quota" response, autoresponders, spam filter requests, or automatically generated ISP notices of nondeliverability.

2. See the American Association for Public Opinion Research, *Standard Definitions: Final Dispositions of Case Codes and Outcome Rates for Surveys*, 5th ed. (Lenexa, KS: AAPOR), 31–32, 35.

3. As discussed more fully below, population targets were based on "adult females and households with own children under 18," because of the absence of reliable distribution data on other scenarios such as adopted or foster children, as well as cases where the household female was not the primary caregiver.

4. It should be noted, however, that sampling error does not take into account other possible sources of error inherent in any study of public opinion, attitudes, interests, or behaviors, particularly when estimates are based on self-reports of "socially desirable" behaviors (such as voting or charitable giving) or "socially undesirable" behaviors (such as drug use or marital infidelity).

Index